99 BISCUITS AND CAKES

MARI LAJOS · KÁROLY HEMZŐ

with **33** COLOUR PHOTOGRAPHS

Corvina

Title of the original: 99 sütemény és torta 33 színes ételfotóval.
Corvina, Budapest, 1986

Translated by Judith Elliott
Consultant: J. Audrey Ellison
Design by Vera Köböl
© Mari Lajos and Károly Hemző, 1987
ISBN 963 13 2308 0
CO 2462–h–8688

On the cover: Coffee cake

Printed in Hungary 1987
Kossuth Printing House, Budapest

PREFACE

Poor king Darius, what he would have given for a cream cake. But it took a long time for the unleavened honey cake with which he was familiar to develop into the sophisticated and enticing works of art that decorate the shelves of confectioners' and bakers' shops today. It is true, of course, that the conquering Moors and Turks played an important part in the development of today's confectionery. The galleys of the Republic of Venice sailed the seas, often plagued by pirates and fierce storms to far off, distant lands, returning with sugar cane to the delight of Europe. At first it was meticulously weighed on precision scales like a medicine, and it competed with the price of the most expensive poisons. The real "revolution" for the confectioner, however, did not come until the introduction of the far cheaper and more easily obtainable sugar beet. This happened quite recently in history, only about 200 years ago, and ever since there has been a feeling of nostalgia for the "Turkish" honey cake and Hansel and Gretel's gingerbread house.

I agree that it is easier, though more expensive, to buy cakes in shops than to bake your own. I can remember very well how my grandmother used to create the most delectable cakes from almost nothing, and for her, it seemed to be the easiest thing in the world. When I think back to those gorgeous vanilla-smelling Sundays of my childhood and then picture the disappointment on the face of a child today when he sees his mother rush into the nearest supermarket to buy a cake for his birthday, I feel how important it is to make things at home. It is not such an exhausting task, there's no magic involved, and children are happy to lend a hand. It is worthwhile hurrying home or staying in to help with the jointly prepared cake. It sweetens childhood memories and the hardships of adult life.

That's all very well, you might say, but how do you go about it? I'll tell you: Take a pinch of courage (if it does not work out the first time, don't give up, try again), a large amount of good humour, some time and patience, a good oven, a few bowls, a wooden spoon, an electric beater and, of course, the ingredients. One basic rule is to weigh the quantities carefully. Always keep a watchful eye on the hand of your assistant in case too few nuts go into the cake, or not enough chocolate. Glance at the APPENDIX before you begin as you might discover some useful tips. Then follow the instructions carefully, step by step. Finally guard the hot cake from pilferers, because they will only end up with stomach aches. And that is really all there is to cake-making.

When planning to bake a sweet dish for a dinner party, make sure that it harmonizes with the menu. Always choose a light sweet after a substantial starter or main course. Do not pressure a guest to eat the sweet that you have prepared or feel offended if he refuses. Your guest might be making a courageous effort to diet and it must be painfully difficult to carry this out anyway without other folk interfering.

The preparation and attractive appearance of a sweet dish is even more important than in the case of other courses. It must be so beautiful and eye-catching that it cannot be resisted even by the guest who feels he is already more than satisfied. This finale, often a non-essential "extra", will be more memorable than the equally delicious courses that preceeded it.

Unless otherwise stated, the quantities in the recipes are for 4 to 6 people. Do not, however, take this as gospel truth because I don't know how sweet-toothed your family or dinner guests are likely to be.

SMALL TEA BISCUITS

Basic recipe

150 g	sugar	5 oz
150 g	butter or margarine	5 oz
2	eggs, separated	2
300 g	plain flour	11 oz
20 g	baking powder	2 tsp
	salt	

Cream together the butter and sugar and beat in the egg yolks until light and frothy. Fold in the sieved flour and baking powder and a pinch of salt. Finally add the stiffly beaten egg whites. Place the mixture into a forcing bag and using a round or star-shaped nozzle press out shapes onto a buttered and floured baking tray. Place in a preheated oven (150–160° C/300–325° F/Gas 2–3 and bake until golden in colour.
Note: The biscuits can be enriched by adding grated orange or lemon rind or approximately 20 g (¾ oz) ground walnuts, hazelnuts or almonds. These biscuits keep extremely well.

Small sandwiched tea biscuits and variations

(for 8 people)

230 g	butter or margarine	8 oz
200 g	icing sugar	7 oz
2	eggs, separated	2
450 g	flour	1 lb
20 g	baking powder	2 tsp
1 tsp	vanilla sugar (see p. 60)	1 tsp
	salt	
1	egg for glazing	1
10 g	butter	2 tsp
for the jam filling		
100 g	sour cherry or apricot jam	4 oz
for the raisin and candied fruit filling		
70 g	raisins or sultanas	3 oz
100 g	candied or crystallized fruit	4 oz
walnut-date filling		
50g	dates	2 oz
25 g	walnuts	1 oz
1 tbs	lemon juice	1 tbs

walnut-honey filling		
30 g	walnuts	1¼ oz
2 tbs	honey	2 tbs

To prepare the biscuits cream the butter and sugar until light and fluffy. Add the lightly beaten eggs and then gradually fold in the flour, baking powder, vanilla sugar and a pinch of salt to make a stiff mixture. Mix thoroughly together, shape into a ball and cover with foil. Leave to rest for 30 minutes. Divide mixture into 4 for the 4 types of sandwiched biscuits.

1. Jam sandwich biscuits
Using a quarter of the mixture, roll it out very thinly and stamp out with a pastry cutter 6–8 cm (2¼–2½ in) in diameter. Place ½ teaspoon of jam in the centre of each round. Brush the edges with a little egg white to stop the jam from oozing out. Sandwich together securely, prick the top with a fork and brush with a little beaten egg. Arrange on a greased baking tray (it should make about 22 biscuits). Place in a preheated oven (180° C/350° F/Gas 4) until golden brown. (About 20 minutes.) Meanwhile prepare the second variation.

2. Sultana and candied fruit biscuits
Soak the sultanas or raisins and drain well. Dice the candied fruit and mix with sultanas. Roll out the mixture and cut into squares 5 × 5 cm (2 × 2 in). Spread a little of the filling in the centre of each square and roll up. Shape into small croissants. Place on a greased baking tray, brush with beaten egg and put into the moderate oven (makes approximately 24 biscuits).

3. Walnut and date biscuits
Roll out the mixture and stamp out with a pastry cutter, roughly 5 cm (2 in) in diameter. Cut out the centre of half the circles with a small round pastry cutter. Chop up the walnuts and dates and mix together, adding half the lemon juice. Place half a teaspoon of the walnut mixture in the centre of the rest of the circles. Place the circles with the holes on top. Press the edges together well, arrange on a greased baking tray and put in the oven when the sultana and candied fruit biscuits are ready (makes approximately 18).

4. Honey and walnut biscuits
Grind the walnuts and mix with the honey, adding a little lemon juice to taste. Roll out the mixture and cut into diamond shapes, roughly 5 cm (2 in) long. Place a little of the filling in the centre of half of the biscuits. Sandwich together pressing the edges firmly. Arrange on a greased baking tray, prick with a fork and brush with beaten egg. Bake until golden brown (makes approximately 16). Sprinkle with a little vanilla icing sugar (see p. 60) while still warm.
When the honey and walnut biscuits have cooled, pile them all on to a large plate.

Note: On first reading, the recipes for the biscuits may seem a formidable task, but in fact, they can all be prepared in about an hour and a half, with some assistance from the children even less, with the added advantage that it will give them a real sense of achievement.

Walnut kisses

(a useful recipe for any left-over egg whites)
for each egg white use

70 g	icing sugar	3 oz
50 g	walnuts	2 oz

Beat the egg white and icing sugar together with a whisk over a pan of hot water. Remove from the heat and continue whisking until thick and soft peaks form between the mixture and the beater. Then mix in the roughly chopped walnuts and arrange on a greased baking tray using half a teaspoonful of the mixture at a time. Place in a preheated oven (130° C/275° F/Gas 1) and bake for 30–35 minutes. The biscuits should rise, turn golden brown and be hollow inside. Walnut kisses are delicious and keep extremely well.
Note: Walnut kisses can also be prepared using almonds or hazelnuts.

Almond rings

(for 6–8 people)

500 g	plain flour	1¼ lb
250 g	castor sugar	9 oz
200 ml	single cream	⅖ pt
9	egg yolks	9
300 g	blanched almonds	11 oz
250 g	butter or margarine	9 oz
50 ml	milk	3 tbs
	grated rind of 2 lemons	
	salt	

Place the flour in a bowl. Make a well in the centre and blend in 8 of the egg yolks, one at a time. Then add the sugar, lemon rind, diced butter, a pinch of salt and the ground almonds (leave 15–20 almond halves aside for chopping as decoration). Mix together thoroughly, then roll out and cut into fingers 15 cm (6 in) in length. Shape into rings, pressing the two ends gently together. Arrange on a greased and floured baking tray. Brush with the remaining egg yolk mixed with a little milk. Sprinkle with the roughly chopped almonds. Put in a preheated oven (180° C/350° F/

Almond rings

Gas 4) and bake for 15–20 minutes until the biscuits are golden brown and the almonds on the top have browned a little. Leave to cool on the tray. Almond rings will keep for a long time if stored in a tin.

Almond-cherry balls

(makes 50—60 biscuits)

200 g	flour	7 oz
15 g	baking powder	½ oz
80 g	icing sugar	3 oz
2	egg yolks	2
150 g	butter or margarine	5 oz
	grated rind of 1 lemon	
	for decoration	
2	egg whites	2
15–20	blanched almonds	15–20
15–20	candied or crystallized cherries	15–20

Mix together the flour, baking powder and sugar in a bowl. Add the egg yolks, the diced butter and lemon rind and beat thoroughly. Shape into a ball, cover with foil and place in the refrigerator for 30 minutes. Meanwhile, halve the blanched almonds using a sharp knife and cut the cherries in half. Make little balls of the mixture, about the size of a walnut and push a piece of almond or cherry into the centre of each ball. Dip them into the lightly beaten egg white and arrange on a greased baking tray at 2 cm (1 in) spacing. If you prefer, whole almonds and cherries can be used to decorate the biscuits.

Bake in a preheated oven (200° C/400° F/Gas 6) for twenty minutes. Allow the biscuits to cool on the tray before arranging on a plate. They keep for a long time if stored in a tin with a tightly fitting lid.

Honey and almond crisps

400 g	blanched almonds	1 lb
250 g	plain flour	9 oz
300 g	honey	11 oz
4	egg whites	4
2 tsp	butter (for greasing)	2 tsp
	salt	

Sieve the flour into a deep bowl, then gradually add the honey, stirring until smooth. If the honey is very thick mix with a little lukewarm water. Split the almonds in half with a sharp knife. Add the almonds and a pinch of salt. Finally lightly fold in the stiffly beaten egg whites. Using a small spoon put little mounds on a greased baking tray at some distance from one another as they rise to at least twice their size during baking. Place in a preheated oven (160°/325° F/Gas 3) and bake for 20–25 minutes until light golden brown. Leave to cool on the baking tray. When eaten fresh they are beautifully crisp, but they are even more delicious if left standing for a few days. Serve with coffee or tea or ice cream.

Vanilla horns

140 g	butter or margarine	5 oz
70 g	castor sugar	3 oz
70 g	walnuts, chopped	3 oz
170 g	plain flour	6 oz
	grated rind of 1 lemon	
	vanilla icing sugar	

Cream the butter and sugar until light and fluffy. Fold in the flour, walnuts and grated lemon rind. If it is too stiff add a little milk. Knead well together, then roll into thick strips. Cut into fingers about 5–6 cm (2–2¼ in) long. Shape into horns. Arrange on a greased floured baking tray and bake

in a preheated oven (160–180° C/325–350° F/Gas 3–4) until golden brown. Dust with vanilla icing sugar while still hot. Shake off the excess sugar. These biscuits will keep for a long time if stored in an airtight container; in fact they become more delicious as time goes by.

Almond croissant supreme

	For the biscuit mixture see Ladies' caprice (p. 18)	
20 g	vanilla sugar (see p. 60)	1 oz
2	eggs	2
100 g	apricot jam	4 oz
200 g	blanched almonds	7 oz
25–30	glacé or crystallized cherries or morello cherries	25–30

Prepare the mixture following the recipe for Ladies' caprice (see p. 18) but add the vanilla sugar or 1 tsp vanilla essence. Roll out on a floured surface and cut into triangles with sides of approximately 10 cm (4 in) long. Spread with a thin layer of apricot jam. Roll up and shape like a croissant. Arrange on a greased, floured baking tray. Cover with a clean kitchen cloth or a sheet of oiled plastic and put aside to rise for 30 minutes. Brush with beaten egg and sprinkle with the roughly chopped almonds. Press a glacé cherry on the top of each croissant. Place in a preheated oven (200° C/400° F/Gas 6) and bake until crisp and rich golden brown. This is a real delicacy and stays delicious for days.

Walnut sponge crescents

3	eggs, separated	3
250 g	plain flour	9 oz
250 g	castor sugar	9 oz
100 g	butter or margarine	4 oz
100 ml	milk	⅕ pt
20 g	baking powder	2 heaped tsp
100 g	walnuts	4 oz
	vanilla icing sugar	

Cream together the 3 egg yolks, sugar and butter until light and fluffy. Then gradually blend in the sieved flour and baking powder and milk, alternating between the two. Finally fold in the stiffly beaten egg whites.

Pour into a greased and floured oblong tin. Sprinkle the top with the roughly chopped walnuts (almonds or hazelnuts are equally good). Place in a preheated oven (180° C/350° F/Gas 4) and bake. (As with all sponge cakes do not open the oven door for the first 20 minutes otherwise the cake will collapse.) When the cake is done, leave it in the tin until nearly cool, then carefully turn out on to a chopping board so that the walnut side is uppermost. Cut into attractive crescent shapes. (Don't worry about the leftover bits, the other members of the family will be enticed into the kitchen by the delicious aroma and those little bits will be snapped up in no time. You will find it hard to resist tasting them yourself.)

Dust the top with vanilla icing sugar (see p. 60).

Witch's scones

	(for 6–8 people)	
250 g	butter or margarine	9 oz
250	castor sugar	9 oz
½	lemon	½
4	eggs, separated	4
80–100 g	walnuts, chopped	3–4 oz
	a little flour	
	jam	

Cream together the butter, sugar, the lemon juice, grated rind and the egg yolks until light and fluffy. Add just enough flour to stop the mixture from sticking to the hands. Form into balls the size of a walnut. Beat the egg whites lightly and add the roughly chopped walnuts. Dip each ball into the

Walnut sponge crescents

egg white and arrange on a greased, floured baking tray. Press the top of each ball with the finger tips. Place in a preheated oven (140–150° C/275–300° F/ Gas 1–2) and bake until pale golden brown. Add a little jam in the well of each biscuit while still hot (sour cherry, strawberry or apricot jam are the best kinds of). This is a particularly delicious biscuit.

Honey kisses

(prepare 1 or 2 days before serving)
(makes approximately 70)

200 g	honey	7 oz
250 g	sugar	9 oz
1 kg	plain flour	2¼ lb
3	eggs, separated	3
20 g	baking powder	2 tsp
30 g	butter	1 oz
200 ml	milk	²/₅ pt
20 g	ammonium bicarbonate	¾ oz
	ground cinnamon	
	grated lemon rind	

Pour the honey into a pan, add 100 ml (⅕ pt) water and bring to the boil. Remove from the heat and stir frequently until cool. Place the flour in a bowl and add the honey. Work together until it resembles bread crumbs. Then blend in the butter, the 3 egg yolks, the baking powder, cinnamon and lemon rind. Finally add the ammonium bicarbonate which has been soaked in lukewarm milk. Knead thoroughly together, form into a ball and leave to rest overnight. Place on a floured surface and roll out very thinly. Stamp out the biscuits using a medium-sized pastry cutter. Arrange on a greased and floured baking tray. Bake in a pre-

Witch's scones

heated oven (200° C/425° F/Gas 7). When cool dip into a white sugar glaze (see p.62). Leave to dry. Store for 1–2 days before eating. They keep very well.

Zebras

(for 6–8 people)

500 g	plain flour	1¼ lb
300 g	sugar	11 oz
300 g	butter or margarine	11 oz
100 g	plain chocolate or	4 oz
2 tbs	cocoa	2 tbs
2	eggs	2
	grated rind of 1 lemon	

Cream together the butter and sugar in a deep bowl. Then gradually blend in the flour and the eggs one at a time and finally the lemon rind. Divide the mixture in half and add the grated chocolate or cocoa to one portion.

Place on a floured surface and roll out both halves to approximately finger thickness. Cut into 10 cm (4 in) long fingers, all the same length. Shape each one into a horseshoe and join a plain one with a chocolate one, either by twisting them loosely together, or pressing one on top of another or facing in opposite directions. Arrange on a greased, floured baking tray and bake in a preheated oven (180° C/350° F/Gas 4) for 20–30 minutes. Leave to cool on the tray. They are extremely attractive to look at and are also very tasty.

Honey biscuits

(makes 60–80 biscuits)

3	eggs	3
100 g	castor sugar	4 oz
350 g	honey	12 oz
50 g	chilled margarine or butter	2 oz
700 g	plain flour	1⅓ lb
1 tsp	bicarbonate of soda	1 tsp
	walnuts or hazelnuts	

Cream together the eggs, sugar, honey and margarine until frothy. Gradually fold in the flour and finally the bicarbonate of soda. Knead together well. Roll out fairly thinly (3–4 mm, less than ¼ in) on a floured surface and stamp out with differently shaped pastry cutters (heart, crescent etc. shapes). Place half a walnut or hazelnut on each biscuit and bake in a preheated oven (200° C/400° F/Gas 6).

Honey kisses

Look at them frequently as they cook very quickly and will taste bitter if overcooked. They will keep for weeks if stored in an airtight tin, in fact the longer they are kept the better they will be. This is an excellent biscuit for breakfast or to take on picnics.

Assorted biscuits

(for 6–8 people)

500 g	plain flour	1¼ lb
250 g	castor sugar	9 oz
200 g	margarine	7 oz
2	eggs	2
20 g	baking powder	2 heaped tsp
20 g	vanilla sugar (see p. 60)	¾ oz
3 tbs	cocoa	3 tbs
	sour cherry or apricot jam	

Mix the flour, baking powder, sugar, vanilla sugar, margarine and eggs to form a fairly stiff mixture. Add a little milk if it is too stiff. Divide into two and add the cocoa to half of the mixture.

Roll out each portion separately until they are approximately 5 mm (¼ in) thick. Stamp out with a round pastry cutter and arrange on a greased and floured baking tray. Bake in a preheated oven

(160–180° C/325–350° F/Gas 3–4) for 20 minutes. When cool, sandwich a chocolate and a plain biscuit together with a little jam. It is best to keep the biscuits for one day before eating. They keep very well in an airtight tin.

Variation: Buttercream flavoured in various ways may be used to sandwich the biscuits together instead of jam.

Snowballs

300 g	plain flour	11 oz
450 g	icing sugar	1 lb
100 g	butter	4 oz
9	eggs	9
½ tsp	cocoa	½ tsp
20 g	vanilla sugar (see p. 60))	1 oz
20 g	baking powder	2 tsp
300 ml	milk	½ pt
50–100 g	dessicated coconut	2–4 oz

Beat 8 of the egg yolks with 350 g (12 oz) of the icing sugar. Gradually add 7 tbs of hot water, then the cocoa, the baking powder and 250 g (9 oz) of the flour, a little at a time. Mix thoroughly together. Finally beat 8 of the egg whites until stiff and fold lightly into the mixture. Pour into 2 greased and floured sandwich tins. Smooth the top and bake in a preheated oven (180° C/350° F/Gas 4) for 25–30 minutes. Allow to cool in the tins.

To make the filling cream the butter with 80 g (3 oz) of the icing sugar until light and fluffy. Put the remaining flour into a separate bowl. Then add the rest of the icing sugar, the vanilla sugar, the whole egg and the milk. Beat until smooth. Place the bowl over boiling water and continue to beat until it thickens. Then put aside to cool. Gradually add to the creamed butter and sugar and beat until frothy.

When the cakes are cool cut circles using a pastry cutter. Spread with the cream, sandwich the circles together. Spread the sides with cream and roll in the dessicated coconut.

These cakes look extremely attractive and should be eaten while fresh. They are quite delicious and are bound to be a success even for the beginner.

Snowballs

"Ischler" biscuits

(a traditional Hungarian biscuit coated with chocolate glaze and filled with jam)

140 g	butter or margarine	5 oz
210 g	plain flour	7 oz
100 g	icing sugar	4 oz
70 g	ground walnuts	3 oz
	grated rind of ½ lemon	
	pinch cinnamon	
	pinch salt	
	jam (preferably apricot)	
for the chocolate glaze		
2 tbsp	sugar	2 tbsp
1 tbs	cocoa	1 tbs
30 g	butter	1 oz

Place all the ingredients, excluding the jam, into a bowl and mix thoroughly together. Form a ball and put aside for 30 minutes. Then roll out to a thickness of 5 mm (¼ in). Cut out circles 5–6 cm (2½–2¾ in) in diameter. Arrange on a greased and floured baking tray and bake in a preheated oven (180° C/350° F/Gas 4) until light golden brown (approximately 10 minutes). When cool, sandwich together with jam and arrange on a cake rack.

To prepare the glaze place the sugar in a pan and add 4 tbs water. Cook until thick. Remove from the heat, add the cocoa and butter and beat until smooth and bubbly. Leave to cool for 2–3 minutes, then spread on both sides of the biscuits. If you want the glaze to look really shiny and smooth, put the glazed biscuits into the oven which has been turned off for 10 minutes, leaving the oven door open.

This is another biscuit which improves with time. They should be prepared 1–2 days before you plan to eat them. This will allow the full flavour of the jam to be absorbed.

Pozsony crescents (walnut and poppyseed)

(makes 30–35 biscuits)

500 g	plain flour	1¼ lb
250 g	butter or margarine	9 oz
15 g	fresh yeast	½ oz
1	egg	1

30 g	sugar	1 oz
	salt	
	cinnamon	
200 ml	milk	⅖ pt
2	sugar lumps	2
	grated rind of 1 lemon	
for the walnut filling		
100 g	sugar	4 oz
100 ml	milk	⅕ pt
200 g	ground walnuts	7 oz
50 g	sultanas	2 oz
for the poppyseed filling		
100 g	sugar	4 oz
200 g	ground poppyseed	7 oz
100 ml	milk	⅕ pt
1 tbs	honey	1 tbs
2–3	chopped cloves	2–3

Leave the yeast to rise in 50 ml (3 tbs) of the slightly warmed milk, adding the sugar lumps if dried yeast is used. Rub the butter into the flour, then add the sugar, a pinch of salt, a pinch of cinnamon and the lemon rind. Finally add the

Walnut and poppyseed crescents

yeast and enough lukewarm milk to make a fairly stiff, elastic dough (the right consistency is reached when the dough comes away from the hands). Form into a ball, cover with a kitchen cloth and leave to rest for 30 minutes at room temperature. Meanwhile prepare the fillings. If you want to make half with poppyseed and half with walnut, then use half the quantities given.

Make both the fillings in the same way – bring the milk and sugar to the boil (with the poppyseed filling add the honey). Blanch the poppyseed and the walnuts in the milk. Add the remaining ingredients, mix well and chill.

Break off pieces of dough, about the size of an egg. Roll each one out fairly thinly. Spread with filling, roll up and shape into croissants or horseshoes. Arrange on a greased and floured baking tray, spaced well apart. Brush the top with a little beaten egg and put in a warm place to rise for 30–40 minutes. Brush again with egg as this will give the cakes a beautiful marbled top. Bake in a preheated oven (200° C/400° F/Gas 6) for about 30 minutes until golden brown. Leave to cool before arranging on a serving plate.

Note: This is a traditional cake of the *belle époque,* evoking images of promenades, brass bands and pump rooms.

Hungarian meltaways

500 g	plain flour	1¼ lb
200 g	butter or margarine	7 ob
20 g	yeast	¾ oz
2	lumps sugar (if dried yeast is used)	2
100 ml	milk	⅕ pt
50 g	icing sugar	2 oz
20 g	vanilla sugar (see p. 60)	¾ oz
	salt	
50–100 ml	soured cream	3–6 tbs

For the filling use apricot jam, ground walnuts, ground poppyseed or chestnut purée with vanilla sugar to taste.

Add the yeast to the lukewarm milk and leave until frothy. Add the sugar lumps if dried yeast is used instead of fresh. Rub the butter into the flour then add the yeast mixture, the icing sugar, vanilla sugar and a pinch of salt. Knead well together to form a fairly stiff dough. Add a little soured cream if necessary. Roll out on a floured surface until approximately 4 mm (⅛ in) thick. Stamp out with a large circular pastry cutter.

Place a teaspoon of filling in the centre of each circle. Moisten the edges with water and fold in

half, pressing the edges gently together. Place on greased and floured baking tray and bake in a preheated oven (180° C/350° F/Gas 4) until light golden brown. Turn in vanilla sugar while still hot.

These are best if put away for 2–3 days before serving.

Jam pockets

(basic recipe)

300 g	plain flour	11 oz
20 g	baking powder	2 tsp
125 g	castor sugar	4½ oz
20 g	vanilla sugar (see p. 60)	¾ oz
	grated rind of ½ lemon	
2	eggs	2
75 g	butter or margarine	3 oz
2 tbs	aniseed liqueur	2 tbs
100–150 g	plum jam	4–5 oz
10 g	butter (for greasing)	2 tsp
	vanilla sugar (for sprinkling)	

Blend together the flour, baking powder, castor sugar, vanilla sugar and lemon rind. Rub in the butter, then add the eggs and liqueur. Mix thoroughly together. Place on a floured surface and roll out to a thickness of approximately 5 mm (½ in). Stamp out with a fluted pastry cutter (8 cm–3¼ in. in diameter). Place a heaped teaspoon of jam in the centre of each round, fold in half and press the edges firmly together. Using a spatula, arrange the jam pockets well apart on a greased and floured baking tray. Bake in a preheated oven (180° C/350° F/Gas 4) for about 20 minutes. Leave to cool on the tray. Sprinkle with a little vanilla sugar. (A little cinnamon can be added to the vanilla sugar if desired.) Pile on to a round plate.

Note: This is really one of the easiest cakes to make and it will always be a success. It keeps very well.

Walnut balls (a Viennese speciality)

(requires no cooking)
(makes 20–25)

200 g	ground walnuts	7 oz
200 g	icing sugar	7 oz
200 g	grated plain chocolate or	7 oz
2 tbs	cocoa	2 tbs
1 tbs	apricot jam	1 tbs
2 tbs	rum	2 tbs

1	egg white	1
	castor sugar	
20–25	bottled morello cherries or morello cherries in rum	20–25
	rice paper	

Put the walnuts, sugar, chocolate, jam, rum and egg white into a bowl and mix thoroughly together. Moisten the hands and shape the mixture into balls about the size of a walnut. Press a cherry into the centre of each ball. Roll in castor sugar and place on rice paper. Leave uncovered in an airy place for 1 or 2 days to dry slightly.
Note: The balls can be rolled in grated chocolate or cocoa powder.

"Dalauzi" (an Armenian speciality)

(makes enough for an army, but it will soon disappear.)

250 g	honey	9 oz
500 g	walnuts	1¼ lb
250 g	poppyseed	9 oz.

Pour the honey into a non-stick pan and cook over a low heat until it has turned red. Test by pouring a few drops on to a wet plate. It is ready if it breaks when cool. Heat the ground poppyseed and ground walnuts in separate pans. Reserve a few walnut halves for decoration. Add first the poppyseed then the walnuts to the honey. Mix well together, leave to stand for a few minutes, then heat in a pan.

Turn on to a clean, oiled surface, spread out until about 1 cm (½ in) thick. Then fold in half. Decorate with walnut halves. When quite cool cut into squares 2 × 2 cm (¾ × ¾ in) with a wet knife. Arrange on a plate and serve quite cold.
Note: They are very rich so do not force yourself to eat more than two. Among eastern peoples this is considered to be a great delicacy, only prepared for special guests. You must accept at least one square, otherwise your host and hostess will be dreadfully offended.

FRUIT CAKES
Hungarian plum cake

125 g	butter or margarine	4½ oz
125 g	castor sugar	4½ oz
2	eggs	2
1	egg yolk	1
100 g	sultanas	4 oz
50 g	candied or crystallized lemon peel	2 oz
2 tbs	rum	2 tbs
	grated rind of 1 lemon	
125 g	plain flour	4½ oz

Soak the sultanas in the rum. Cream the butter and sugar in a large bowl until light and fluffy. Beat in the eggs and egg yolk one at a time. Drain the sultanas and turn in a little flour. Then add the sultanas, the diced lemon peel (any other candied or glacé fruit can be used if preferred), the rum, the greated rind and finally the flour.

Turn into a greased, lined oblong cake tin. Smooth the top and bake in a preheated oven (180° C/ 350° F/Gas 4) until golden brown and the top begins to crack. Test with a meat skewer, if the skewer comes out clean after inserting into the cake, it is ready. (Remember not to open the oven door for the first 30 minutes otherwise the cake will sink.) Leave to cool in the tin. Turn out on to a plate and cut into fingers.

These delicious cakes go very well with tea and will be a favourite with the whole family.

Hungarian ginger bread

125 g	butter	4½ oz
150 g	icing sugar	5 oz
2	eggs	2
220 g	plain flour	8 oz
½ tsp	bicarbonate of soda	½ tsp
½ tsp	cinnamon	½ tsp
1 tsp	ginger	1 tsp
½ tsp	nutmeg	½ tsp
250 ml	milk	½ pt
	whipped cream	

Cream the butter and sugar until light and fluffy, then beat in the eggs one at a time. Mix together the flour, bicarbonate of soda, cinnamon, ginger and nutmeg in a separate bowl. Pour the vinegar into the milk and then add to the egg mixture, alternating with the flour. Grease and line a square tin with

sides about 20 cm (8 in) long and 5 cm (2 in) deep. Pour in the mixture, smooth the top and bake in a preheated oven (180° C/350° F/Gas 4) for approximately 1 hour. (Do not open the oven door for the first 30 minutes otherwise the cake will collapse.) Leave in the tin for 10–15 minutes before turning out on to a plate. Serve while still slightly warm. Top with whipped cream.

Note: This ginger bread is probably of English or Indian origin. It is now very popular in many parts of the world, including America and Hungary, of course. It has a particularly good flavour because of all the spices.

Bishop's bread

120 g	butter or margarine	4½ oz
140 g	sugar	5 oz
140 g	plain flour	5 oz
6	eggs, separated	6
120 g	mixture of walnuts, almonds, quince cheese, plain chocolate and candied orange peel	4½ oz
	salt	
	vanilla icing sugar or chocolate glaze	

Cream the butter and sugar until light and fluffy, then beat in the 6 egg yolks, a little at a time. Add the nuts, quince cheese etc. to the flour, then fold lightly into the egg mixture. Add a pinch of salt to the egg whites and beat until stiff, then fold in very slightly. Pour into a greased and floured, fluted oblong or round tin. Bake in a preheated oven (140° C/275° F/Gas 1) for 50–60 minutes. Leave to cool in the tin. Turn out onto a plate and dust with vanilla icing sugar (see p. 60), or cover with a chocolate glaze (see p. 63). Cut into thin slices and serve with tea or ice-cream.

Cream slice

(it is good for using up left-over egg whites)

6	egg whites	6
160 g	icing sugar	6 oz
2 g	vanilla sugar (see p. 60)	1 oz
80 g	butter	3 oz
160 g	plain flour	6 oz
	grated rind of 1 lemon	
30 g	almonds	1 oz

Melt the butter. Beat the egg whites until stiff then fold in a little at a time the sugar, the melted but not hot butter, the vanilla sugar, the lemon rind, grated almonds and finally the flour. Pour into a greased and floured fluted oblong tin or ring tin. Smooth the top and bang the bottom of tin gently to remove any air bubbles. Bake in a preheated oven (140° C/275° F/Gas 1) for 45–60 minutes until light golden brown and the top begins to crack slightly. Test by inserting a meat skewer into the centre of the cake. If it comes out clean the cake is done.

Leave to cool in the tin. Cut into thin slices and serve with ice-cream, tea or cocoa.

It keeps very well if stored in an airtight tin or wrapped in kitchen foil. It is one of many types of cakes, not spectacular to look at but definitely delicious to eat.

Note: This sweet can look more attractive if covered with a chocolate glaze (see p. 63).

Notes

_____
_____
_____
_____
_____
_____
_____
_____
_____
_____
_____
_____
_____
_____
_____
_____
_____
_____
_____
_____
_____
_____
_____
_____
_____
_____

Bishop's bread

RICH CREAM CAKES AND SWEETS

Mother's tart

(for 6–8 people)

500 g	plain flour	1¼ lb
250 g	butter or margarine	9 oz
20 g	yeast	¾ oz
2	eggs	2
100 g	castor sugar	4 oz
	salt	
	a little milk	
	grated rind of 1 lemon	

Mix the flour, sugar and lemon rind in a bowl. Rub in the fresh yeast, then add the butter. Blend thoroughly together before adding one egg and a pinch of salt. The dough should be fairly stiff and elastic. Add a little lukewarm milk if necessary. The dough can be divided into two or more parts depending on what you plan to make with it. Roll out on a floured surface to a thickness of approximately 4 mm (scant ¼ in) and with the help of a rolling pin place on to a greased and floured baking tray. You may spread any filling you wish on to the dough (curd cheese, fresh or bottled fruit, walnuts, poppyseed, etc). Put another piece of dough on top and press the edges firmly. Leave in a warm place to rise for at least 30 minutes. Prick the top with a fork and brush with beaten egg. Place in a preheated oven (180° C/350° F/Gas 4) for approximately 25 minutes or until golden brown. Leave in the tray to cool and slice as desired.

Note: If you want a beautiful "cracked" effect on the top, brush the dough twice with beaten egg —once immediately after preparing it, and the second time just before baking. The tart looks very nice with icing sugar dusted on the top, but it is not essential and it does add extra calories.

Cream squares

(for 6–8 people)

	for the pastry	
100 g	castor sugar	4 oz
2	eggs	2
10 g	vanilla sugar (see p. 60)	1 oz
100 g	plain flour	4 oz
30 g	cornflour	1 oz
	salt	

	for the cream	
70 g	butter	2½ oz
40 g	icing sugar	1½ oz
1	egg yolk	1
150 ml	aromatic liqueur	¼ pt
50 g	jam	2 oz
200 g	cooking chocolate	7 oz

Beat the eggs with the sugar, vanilla sugar and a pinch of salt. Blend in the flour and cornflour. Grease a baking tray approximately 40×20 cm ($15¾ \times 7¾$ in) in size. Pour in the cake mixture and bake for 15–20 minutes in a preheated oven (180° C/350° F/Gas 4). Leave the cake in the tin for a few minutes, then turn it out on to a cake rack and leave to cool.

In the meantime prepare the cream: Cream the butter and sugar, the egg yolk and 1 or 2 tablespoons of the liqueur. Beat until light and fluffy. When the cake is quite cold cut it into two layers. Sprinkle the inside with 100 ml (⅕ pt) of the liqueur. Coat the bottom layer with the cream and cover with the other half. Press gently together. Mix the remaining liqueur with the jam and spread on the top. Put in the refrigerator for about 1 hour, remove the edges and cut into squares. Decorate the top with the melted chocolate, leaving a thin strip of cake visible, because it looks more attractive like that. A piece of candied orange peel or other fruit can be placed in the middle.

Keep chilled until served.

It is very delicious, but should be eaten while fresh. This should not create any difficulty because it is bound to be a great success with everyone.

Poppyseed sandwich cake

(for 6–8 people)

2	eggs	2
100 g	butter or margarine	4 oz
300 g	castor sugar	10 oz
300 ml	ground poppyseed	½ pt
150 g	plain flour	5 oz
300 ml	milk	½ pt
20 g	baking powder	2 tsp
	pinch ground cinnamon	
100 g	red currant or raspberry jam	4 oz
	vanilla sugar (see p. 60)	

Cream the butter and sugar until light and fluffy. Then beat in the eggs. Add the flour and poppyseed a little at a time, alternating with the milk. Lastly mix in the baking powder and the cinnamon. Mix thoroughly together. Pour into a greased and floured tin, measuring approximately 20 × 30 cm (8 × 12 in). Bake in a preheated oven (180° C/350° F/Gas 4) for about 40 minutes. Use a meat skewer to test if the cake is done.

Leave to cool in the tin. Turn out, cut into two layers and spread with the jam. Place the layers together again, pressing them slightly. Put aside for 1 hour to allow the cake to absorb some of the jam. Cut into squares and arrange on a plate. Dust the top with a little vanilla sugar.

Note: This is bound to become a family favourite as it is quick and simple, inexpensive and definitely foolproof.

Chocolate and walnut squares

(for 8 people)

250 g	plain flour	9 oz
120 g	butter or margarine	4½ oz
100 g	plain chocolate	4 oz
80 g	castor sugar	3 oz
1	egg	1
16	walnut halves	16
20 g	baking powder	2 tsp
	flour	
	salt	
	vanilla sugar (see p. 60)	

Break the chocolate into small pieces. Put into a bowl and melt over boiling water. Then put aside to cool slightly. Mix the flour, sugar, baking powder and a pinch of salt in a bowl. Rub in the butter and add the melted chocolate and the egg. Mix together thoroughly. Place on a floured surface

Poppyseed sandwich cake

and roll out to fit a rectangular cake tin (approximately 20 × 30 cm (8 × 12 in). Grease the tin and dust with flour. Place cake mixture in the tin and using a pastry wheel mark into 4 cm (1½ in) squares. Place a walnut half in the middle of each square. Bake in a preheated oven (180° C/350° F/Gas 4) for about 25 minutes. Then while hot use the pastry wheel to divide the cake into squares, cutting down to the bottom of the tin. Leave to cool in the tin.

Arrange on a square plate and dust the top with a little vanilla sugar. Serve with tea or coffee.

Ladies' caprice

300 g	flour	11 oz
200 ml	milk	²/₅ pt
30 g	yeast	1 oz
2	cubes of sugar	2
150 g	butter or margarine	5 oz
30 g	sugar	1 oz
	grated rind of 1 lemon	
5	egg yolks	5
for the filling		
200 g	apricot jam	7 oz
5	egg whites	5
200 g	icing sugar	7 oz
80–100 g	walnuts	3–4 oz

To make the yeast liquid: place the fresh yeast in a bowl with 3 tablespoons of the milk (and the sugar lumps if dried yeast is used) and a little of the flour (see p.). Cream the butter and sugar until light and fluffy, then add the egg yolks, the grated lemon rind, and the yeast mixture. Heat the rest of the milk until lukewarm, blend in the remaining flour and then add to the yeast mixture. Knead well together. Roll out on a floured surface into a rectangle with a thickness of 5 mm (¼ in). Place in a buttered and floured baking tray and press into the corners. Cover with a kitchen cloth and leave in a warm place to rise. Bake in a preheated

Ladies' caprice

Rákóczi curd-cheese meringue squares

oven (200–220° C/400–425° F/Gas 6–7) until it is half-cooked and lightly golden brown. Remove from the oven, spread with the apricot jam, the stiffly beaten icing sugar and egg whites and the roughly chopped walnuts. Return to the oven and bake until the meringue is golden brown. Remove from oven and cut into squares with a wet knife. Do not dust with icing sugar.

Rákóczi curd-cheese meringue squares

(for 8–10 people)

240 g	plain flour	8½ oz
120 g	butter or margarine	4½ oz
60 g	castor sugar	2 oz
1	egg yolk	1
100 ml	soured cream	⅕ pt
	salt	
2 heaped tsp	baking powder	2 heaped tsp
	grated rind of 1 lemon	
for the filling		
500 g	cow's curd-cheese	1 lb 2 oz
100 g	castor sugar	4 oz
3	eggs, separated	3
	salt	
50 g	sultanas or raisins	2 oz
	breadcrumbs	
for the topping		
3	egg whites	3
120 g	icing sugar	4½ oz
	apricot jam	

Put the dry ingredients and lemon rind into a bowl. Rub in the butter and add the egg yolk and soured cream to make a soft pastry. Grease a square or oblong cake tin and dust with flour. Roll out the pastry to a thickness of 1 cm (½ in) and place in the tin. Prick with a fork and bake blind in a preheated oven (180° C/350° F/Gas 4) until half-cooked and very light golden brown. Meanwhile soak the sultanas for a few minutes in water, then drain thoroughly. Mash the curd cheese and beat until light and fluffy with the 3 egg yolks and the sugar. Add the sultanas. Whisk the egg whites with a pinch of salt until stiff, then fold lightly into the curd-cheese mixture. Sprinkle the top of the pastry with about half a handful of breadcrumbs. Smooth on the filling and return to the oven until the pastry is quite cooked.

For the topping beat the egg whites with the sugar until stiff. Put into a forcing bag and make a trellis pattern with a plain nozzle. Return to the oven for one or two minutes until the egg white is a pale fawn colour.

Leave to cool in the tin. Spread apricot jam in between the trellis. Cut into squares with a wet knife.

Note: The cake did not actually get its name from the Hungarian leader Ferenc Rákóczi, but from a famous cook of the same name.

Walnut cream slice

(for 6–8 people)

8	eggs yolks	8
210 g	icing sugar	7 oz
150 g	plain flour	5 oz
5	egg whites	5
	salt	
	for the cream	
2	eggs	2
2	egg yolks	2
150 g	sugar	5 oz
150 g	ground walnuts	5 oz
200 g	butter or margarine	7 oz
2 tbs	rum	2 tbs
	for the glaze	
1	egg	1
150 g	castor sugar	5 oz
	juice of ½ lemon	
	a few walnuts	

To prepare the cake beat the egg yolks and sugar, then add the sieved flour. Beat the egg whites with a pinch of salt until stiff. Fold lightly into the cake mixture. Divide into five, and pour into five small oblong cake tins that have been greased and dusted with flour.

To make the cream beat the eggs and egg yolks with the sugar in a bowl over boiling water until it thickens. Remove from the heat and when cool add the halved walnuts. Beat the butter in a separate bowl until soft and creamy, then add to the cold cream. Finally pour in the rum. Spread a thin layer of cream on each cake. Put the layers together and cover with the *glaze*.

To prepare the glaze beat the egg, sugar and lemon juice together. Arrange the walnut halves on top of the cake and smooth on the glaze. Leave in a cold place for one day.

Cut into squares or wedges using a wet knife.

Note: The origin of this cake is uncertain. I came across it in a small village in the Bakony mountains of Hungary, where a wedding was taking place and the women had just placed this lovely cake on the table. It is thanks to their cooperation that this recipe has become one of my favourites.

Elizabeth's economical lemon cake

(an excellent way of using left-over egg whites)

4	egg whites	4
120 g	icing sugar	4½ oz
	grated rind of 1 lemon	
80 g	plain flour	3 oz
30 g	butter or margarine	1 oz
	salt	

Beat the egg whites in a large bowl with a pinch of salt until stiff. Mix the flour, icing sugar and lemon rind together and fold carefully into the egg whites. Melt the butter and leave to cool before adding to the mixture.

Grease a fluted, oblong cake tin and dust with flour. Pour the cake mixture into the tin, which should be two-thirds full. Bake in a preheated oven (150° C/300° F/Gas 2) for 45–50 minutes. Do not open the oven door for the first 30 minutes, otherwise the cake will collapse. Leave to cool in the tin, then turn out on to an oblong plate.

This cake can be covered with a chocolate glaze but it is equally nice without. Put aside for one day before eating. It keeps extremely well.

Serve with coffee, tea or ice-cream.

Honey sandwich cake

50 g	butter or margarine	2 oz
100 g	icing sugar	4 oz
2	eggs	2
400	plain flour	1 lb
1 tsp	bicarbonate of soda	1 tsp
1 tbs	honey	1 tbs
	for the cream	
500 ml	milk	1 pt
120 g	plain flour	4½ oz
200 g	butter or margarine	7 oz
250 g	icing sugar	9 oz
20 g	vanilla sugar (see p. 60)	1 oz
1	egg	1

Cream together the icing sugar, margarine and honey in a bowl over boiling water. While still hot add the flour, the eggs, and bicarbonate of soda. Mix thoroughly together, divide into 3 balls, then roll out into equal rectangles. Arrange on greased and floured baking trays and bake in a preheated oven (180° C/350° F/Gas 4) for 10–12 minutes until very light golden brown.

To prepare the cream: Place the flour in a bowl and gradually add the milk. Beat until smooth. Heat over a pan of boiling water or in a double saucepan. Cook until it thickens. Remove from the heat and leave to cool, stirring occasionally to prevent a skin from forming on the top. Meanwhile cream together the margarine, sugar, vanilla sugar and the egg until light and fluffy. Then add a little at a time to the cold custard. Sandwich the pastry layers together with the cream.

A *chocolate glaze* can be spread on the top if desired (see p. 63).

It is best to prepare this cake a day before it is required.

Honey sandwich cake

Snow squares

250 g	plain flour	9 oz
20 g	ammonium bicarbonate	1 oz
3 tbs	milk	3 tbs
70 g	butter	3 oz
50 g	icing sugar	2 oz
1	egg	1
	for the cream	
400 ml	milk	¾ pt
80 g	plain flour	3 oz
200 g	butter or margarine	7 oz
200 g	icing sugar	7 oz
20 g	vanilla sugar (see p. 60)	1 oz

Put the ammonium bicarbonate into lukewarm milk and leave to work. Rub the butter into the flour. Add the icing sugar, the egg and the raising agent. Mix well together. Shape into two balls then roll each one out into a rectangle. Arrange on greased and floured baking trays and bake in a preheated oven (180° C/350° F/Gas 4) for 10–12 minutes until light golden brown. Take great care as the pastry breaks very easily. The raising agent will give quite a strong smell to the cake, but do not worry, it will soon disappear and certainly won't spoil the heavenly result.

While the pastry is cooking, *prepare the cream:* Put the flour into a bowl and gradually add the milk, beating until smooth. Cook over a pan of boiling water or in a double saucepan until thick, stirring all the time. Put aside to cool. Cream the butter, vanilla sugar and icing sugar until light and fluffy, then add to the cold custard. Sandwich the pastry with the cream. Dust the top with some extra icing sugar. Prepare at least one day in advance. Keep in a cold place, wrapped carefully in paper.

Note: Baking powder may be used instead of ammonium bicarbonate. Omit steeping the baking powder in lukewarm milk.

Caramel slices

(for 8–10 people)

700 g	plain flour	1½ lb
100 g	icing sugar	4 oz
200 g	castor sugar	7 oz
350 g	margarine	12 oz
1	egg	1
	bicarbonate of soda	
1 l	milk	2 pt

Mix 500 g (1 lb) of the flour with the icing sugar in a bowl. Rub in the margarine, add the egg, 2 good pinches of bicarbonate of soda and enough milk to make a soft pliable pastry. Shape into four balls. Roll out into four rectangles of equal size and approximately 3 mm (¼ in) thick. Arrange on greased and floured baking trays and bake in a preheated oven (180° C/350° F/Gas 4) until light brown. Turn out on to a kitchen cloth.

While the pastry cooks *prepare the cream:* Brown 10 g (4 oz) of the castor sugar in a non-stick pan. Add 350 ml (¾ pt) of the milk and, stirring frequently, bring to the boil. Put the remaining sugar and flour into a bowl and blend in 350 ml (¾ pt) of the milk. Beat until smooth, then add to the hot caramel in the pan. Return to heat and cook until it thickens, stirring constantly. Remove from the heat, stirring frequently as it cools to prevent a skin from forming on the top. When cool beat in the rest of the margarine (250 g–9 oz) until fluffy. Sandwich the 5 layers of pastry with the cream, leaving some for the top.

Put aside for about 9 hours for the pastry to soften and absorb some of the cream. Serve cut into thick slices. They will keep for several days.

Coconut roll

400 g	plain flour	1 lb
250 g	butter or margarine	9 oz
4	eggs, separated	4
300 g	castor sugar	11 oz
10 g	yeast	½ oz
1	lump of sugar (if dried yeast is used)	1
3 tbs	milk	3 tbs
1 tsp	baking powder	1 tsp
	for the cream	
	salt	
100 g	dessicated coconut	4 oz

To make the yeast liquid warm the milk and add the yeast (and sugar lump). Put the flour and baking powder into a bowl, rub in the butter, then add the 4 egg yolks and the yeast liquid. Knead well. Divide into 3 equal portions and shape into balls. Cover and leave in a warm place.

In the meantime prepare the cream: Whisk the egg whites with a pinch of salt until stiff, then lightly fold in the sugar and coconut. Divide into 3. Roll out the dough on a floured surface into 3 equal rectangles. Spread with the filling and roll up very tightly. Cut into slices 5 cm (2 in) thick. Arrange on a greased and floured baking tray some distance apart as they will rise during baking. Bake in a preheated oven (180° C/350° F/Gas 4) for 35–40 minutes. Leave to cool in the baking tray. The top may be dusted with icing sugar if you wish.

DEEP-FRIED CAKES

Sultana and almond doughnuts

60 g	cornflour	2 oz
2 heaped tsp	baking powder	2 heaped tsp
	salt	
250 ml	milk	½ pt
1 tbs	oil	1 tbs
30 g	sultanas	1¼ oz
3 tbs	rum	3 tbs
60 g	blanched almonds	2 oz
1	egg	1
20 g	icing sugar	1 oz
	grated rind of ½ lemon	
80 g	plain flour	3 oz
	a little vanilla sugar (see p. 60)	
	oil for frying	

Put the sultanas in a small bowl, cover with the rum and leave to soak. Place the cornflour, baking powder and a pinch of salt in a large bowl. Blend in enough milk to make a pancake batter consistency. Add the oil, then cover with a cloth. Put aside for 2–3 hours in a cool place. In the meantime drain the sultanas, then shred the almonds and stir fry in a little oil until golden. When the pancake batter has "rested" beat in the egg, the icing sugar and lemon rind, and blend thoroughly. Finally fold in the flour, sultanas and almonds. The batter should be quite thick and glutinous. If it is too thin, add a little more flour. Heat some oil in a pan approximately 3 cm (1½ in) deep. (It would be wise at this stage to open all the windows or turn the extractor fan on full.) With the help of 2 teaspoons, form the batter into balls, roughly the size of a walnut and fry a few at a time in the hot oil. Fry on both sides until golden brown. Drain on kitchen paper or on a cake rack. Dust with vanilla sugar while still hot.
Serve slightly warm. These doughnuts are not so nice if allowed to get cold.

Crispy doughnut twists

250 g	plain flour	9 oz
50 g	castor sugar	2 oz
	salt	
	grated rind of ½ lemon	
2 tsp	baking powder	2 tsp
25 g	butter	1 oz
1	egg	1
1	egg yolk	1
1–2 tbs	spiced white wine	1–2 tbs
	vanilla sugar (see p. 60)	
	oil for deep frying	

Place the flour, baking powder, sugar, a pinch of salt and the grated lemon rind in a bowl. Rub in the butter, then add the egg, egg yolk and the wine. Mix thoroughly together. It should be a fairly stiff pastry. Roll out on a floured surface until thin. Tidy the edges with a pastry wheel, then cut into strips 2 cm × 5 cm (½ in × 2 in). Make two 1 cm (¼ in) slashes in the middle of each strip with a knife. Carefully thread the end of each strip through the slashes, putting each end in the cut furthest away.
Heat some oil in a pan and fry a few at a time on both sides until golden brown. Drain on kitchen paper and leave to cool. Dust with vanilla icing sugar.
This biscuit is at its best when fresh, so don't make more than what you will need.

"Able Mama" (a Transylvanian Armenian speciality)

(for 12–16 people)

1½ kg	plain flour	3½ lb
4	egg yolks	4
1	egg	1
	salt	
50 g	castor sugar	2 oz
100 g	butter or margarine	4 oz
30 g	yeast	1¼ oz
3 tbs	milk	3 tbs
2	lumps of sugar (if dry yeast is used)	2
	a little soured cream	
	plum jam heated and mixed with a little red wine	

"Able Mama"—a Transylvanian Armenian speciality

	vanilla sugar (see p. 60)	
	oil for deep frying	

To prepare the yeast liquid: Put the yeast (and sugar lumps) into a bowl and add the lukewarm milk. Sieve the flour into a bowl, add the yeast and enough water to make a pliable dough. Place in a floured bowl, cover with a kitchen towel and leave to rise in a warm place.

Cream the butter and sugar until light and fluffy, then beat in the egg yolks, the egg and a pinch of salt. Mix thoroughly with the dough and add enough milk or soured cream to make a very soft dough.

Heat some oil in a large pan. Form the dough into balls, about the size of a walnut, and fry a few at a time in the oil. Turn the doughnuts over so that they are light golden brown all over. Drain on kitchen paper. Pile on to a plate and dust with vanilla icing sugar. Serve with hot plum jam diluted with a little red wine in a separate jug or bowl.

Note: You will need quite a lot of time and patience to make these Transylvanian doughnuts, but they are really very delicious.

Candied delight (a Sicilian speciality)

150 g	plain flour	5 oz
1 tbs	honey	1 tbs
1 tbs	castor sugar	1 tbs
3 tbs	sweet white wine	3 tbs
	salt	
	oil for deep frying	
	for the filling	
500 g	curd cheese	1¼ lb
250 g	icing sugar	9 oz
50 g	plain chocolate	2 oz
50 g	a mixture of candied or glacé fruit	2 oz
	pistachio nuts or almonds	

Place the flour, a pinch of salt and the sugar in a bowl. Then add the honey and the white wine. Mix thoroughly, form into a ball and put aside for 30 minutes. Roll out on a floured surface to a thickness of approximately 5 mm (¼ in). Cut into 8 cm (3 in) squares. Roll round small fireproof rods and fry in hot oil until golden brown. Drain on kitchen paper and remove the rods.

Press the curd cheese through a hair sieve or mash finely. Add the icing sugar, the grated chocolate, the chopped fruit and nuts and fill the rolls. Serve cold.

Note: This is a real delicacy, which was probably introduced into Sicily during Arab occupation. The addition of sugar must have come much later. In Sicily today it is not considered out of the ordinary and is sold in the most modest cafés and markets.

Notes

_____
_____
_____
_____
_____
_____
_____
_____
_____
_____
_____
_____
_____
_____
_____
_____
_____
_____
_____
_____
_____
_____
_____
_____
_____
_____
_____
_____

SWEETS MADE WITH YEAST

Basic recipe for sweet leavened dough

(for 6–8 people)

500 g	plain flour	1¼ lb
400 ml	milk	¾ pt
20 g	yeast	1 oz
2	egg yolks	2
50 g	butter	2 oz
50 g	castor sugar	2 oz
	salt	
	grated lemon rind	
2 cubes	sugar (if dried yeast is used)	2 cubes

The secret of success with leavened sweets and bread is that all ingredients, with the exception of milk, should be kept at room temperature for 10–12 hours prior to using. To make the yeast liquid: cream the yeast (it should be very fresh) with the sugar lumps and 3 tablespoons of milk. Pour into a small bowl and mix in enough flour to make a soft dough. Mix thoroughly together using a wooden spoon. Shape the dough into a ball, sprinkle with flour, cover with a kitchen towel and leave in a warm place to double in size. Sieve the remaining flour into a bowl, add the soft dough and knead well. Warm the rest of the milk slightly, add the sugar and salt and stir until dissolved. Mix the egg yolks and the grated lemon rind. Add to the dough, a little at a time. Finally add the melted butter. Knead the dough thoroughly until it blisters and leaves the sides of the bowl clean. Kneading the dough well is another secret to success.

Shape the dough into a ball again, sprinkle with flour, cover with a cloth and leave to rise to double its size (approximately 3 hours) in a warm place. (Never put it directly on a hot plate or radiator.) When the dough has risen follow the chosen recipe.

The final secret of success lies in the *baking*. The oven should be fairly hot (200–220° C/400–425° F/Gas 6–7). If the oven is any hotter, the dough will rise at the beginning but will collapse during baking; if the temperature is lower, the dough will not rise, it will be hard and have a close, heavy texture.

Note: Only choose recipes that require kneading if you have the patience and the time to do it correctly. You need to allow 3–4 hours including the baking time, but don't be discouraged by this.

If fresh or frozen yeast is not available, use half the quantity of dried yeast and add a sugar cube or two when reconstituting the yeast in tepid liquid.

Ferdinand's slices

(for 6–8 people)

350 g	plain flour	12 oz
2	egg yolks	2
30 g	yeast	1¼ oz
1	sugar lump (if dried yeast is used)	1
30 g	icing sugar	1 oz
3 tbs	milk	3 tbs
2 tsp	butter	2 tsp
	salt	
for the filling		
100 g	butter	4 oz
100 g	icing sugar	4 oz
40 g	vanilla sugar (see p. 60)	1½ oz
1	egg yolk	1
3 tbs	sweetened milk	3 tbs

Cream the yeast with the sugar lump and luke-warm milk and leave to ferment. Rub the butter into the flour, then add the sugar, the egg yolks, a pinch of salt and the yeast liquid. Mix well together and add enough milk to make a soft dough.

To prepare the filling cream the butter, icing sugar and vanilla sugar until light and fluffy. Roll out the dough until thin, then spread with the filling. Roll up the dough like a Swiss roll and with a sharp knife cut slices about 1 cm (½ in) thick. Arrange on a greased and floured baking tray a good distance apart because they will double in size. Brush the top with the beaten egg yolk and leave to rise for 1 hour. Bake in a preheated oven (200–220° C/400–425° F/Gas 6–7) until golden brown. Brush with sweetened milk and return to the oven for 1–2 minutes to give the top a beautiful shine. Serve cold, dusted with icing sugar.

Hungarian buns and variations

(for 6–8 people)

300 g	plain flour	11 oz
200 ml	milk	⅖ pt
2	egg yolks	2
10 g	yeast	½ oz

2	lumps of sugar (if dried yeast is used)	2 lumps
40 g	butter	1½ oz
50 g	castor sugar	2 oz
	salt	
	for the top	
40 g	butter	1½ oz
1	beaten egg yolk	1
	vanilla icing sugar (see p. 60)	
	for the jam filling	
200 g	plum, apricot or other jam	7 oz
	for the curd cheese filling	
250–300 g	curd cheese	9–11 oz
50 g	sultanas	2 oz
1	egg yolk	1
	grated rind of 1 lemon	
50 g	icing sugar	2 oz
	for the walnut or poppyseed filling	
100–150 g	ground walnuts or poppyseed	4–5 oz

50 g	castor sugar	2 oz
	grated rind of 1 lemon	
30 g	sultanas	1 oz
1	egg white	1

Make a dough in the usual way (see p. 26). Place on a floured surface, roll and cut into squares approximately 8 cm (3 in) square and 5 mm (¼ in) thick. Spread a teaspoonful of one of the fillings along one edge of each square, then roll up. Arrange on a greased and floured baking tray, in rows. Brush the sides with melted butter, cover with a kitchen cloth and leave to rise. Brush the top with beaten egg yolk, then bake in a preheated oven (200–220° C/400–425° F/Gas 6–7) till golden brown. Leave to cool in the tray, break apart, arrange on a plate and dust with vanilla sugar.

Variations: For curd-cheese filling, beat all ingredients until light and fluffy poppyseed or walnut filling, fold in the stiffly beaten egg at the end.

Hungarian buns and variations

Golden dumplings

	(for 6–8 people)	
300 g	plain flour	11 oz
3	egg yolks	3
30 g	butter or margarine	1 oz
20 g	yeast	1 oz
2	lumps of sugar (if dried yeast is used)	2
30 g	icing sugar	1 oz
250 ml	milk	½ pt
1 tbs	rum	1 tbs
	salt	
	for the filling	
80 g	butter or margarine	3 oz
100 g	ground walnuts	4 oz
50 g	icing sugar	2 oz
50 g	sultanas	2 oz
	grated rind of 1 lemon	
	breadcrumbs	
1	egg yolk	1
	vanilla sugar for dusting (see p. 60)	

Make the dough in the usual way, following the method on page 26 and leave to rise. Put the sultanas in a small bowl with some water to soak. Place the risen dough on a floured surface and pat out by hand, rather than rolling, until the dough is approximately 1 cm (½ in) thick. Stamp out with a pastry cutter 5 cm (2 in) in diameter. Grease a large fireproof dish or round cake tin, one which will hold about 2–2½ litres (3–3¾ pints) of liquid. Sprinkle with breadcrumbs.

Drain the sultanas well. Mix the ground walnuts, icing sugar and grated lemon rind in a bowl. Melt the butter and into it dip each round of dough "dumpling". Turn in the walnut mixture and arrange a layer in the bottom of the fireproof dish. Sprinkle with a few of the sultanas. Then add another layer of dough until all the ingredients are used up, finishing with a layer of dough. Sprinkle with any remaining butter, cover with a kitchen cloth, and leave to rise in a warm place until the dough has almost reached the rim of the dish. Brush with the beaten egg yolk and bake in a preheated oven (200–220° C/ 400–425° F/Gas 6–7) for about 35 minutes until golden brown. Leave to cool in the dish, then turn out on to a serving dish and sprinkle with vanilla icing sugar.

Serve either slightly warm or cold with a wine sauce (see p. 63) or jam.

Rose cake

500 g	plain flour	1¼ lb
2	eggs	2
1	egg yolk	1
40 g	butter	1½ oz
50 g	icing sugar	2 oz
	salt	
35 g	yeast	1½ oz
2	lumps of sugar (if dried yeast is used)	2
100 ml	milk	⅕ pt
	grated lemon rind	
20 g	vanilla sugar (see p. 60)	2 tsp
	for the cream	
100 g	castor sugar	4 oz
100 g	butter	4 oz

Cream the yeast with the sugar lumps and 3 tablespoons of lukewarm milk. Then add 100 g (4 oz) of the flour, shape into a ball and place on a floured surface or in a bowl. Cover with a cloth and leave to rise until double its size. Put the remaining flour in a bowl with the sugar and a pinch of salt. Make a well in the centre and add the eggs, the egg yolk, the butter and grated lemon rind a little at a time. Mix thoroughly together. Finally add the risen dough and knead well. It should be a soft dough. A little lukewarm milk can be added if necessary.

Turn on to a well floured surface and roll out until approximately ½ cm (¼ in) thick and rectangular in shape. *To make the cream* beat the castor sugar and butter until light and fluffy. Spread on the dough and roll up loosely from the long side. Cut the roll into pieces 3–4 cm (1½–2 in) long (it should make about 14). Stand them up in a greased and floured, round cake tin. Press the bottoms slightly so that the cream does not come out and put them a little distance apart. Cover with a kitchen cloth and leave to rise in a warm place until the rose-shaped cakes have "grown" together. Bake in a preheated hot oven (200–220° C/ 400–425° F/Gas 6–7) for approximately 50 minutes. Test with a meat skewer to see if the middle is cooked. Dissolve the vanilla sugar in the rest of the milk and brush the tops and sides of the cakes. Then return to the oven for a further 5 minutes until they turn a beautiful golden brown.

Leave to cool in the cake tin, then turn out on to a plate and serve.

Note: This is one variation of the traditional Hungarian cake called a "wasp's nest", but it looks much more attractive. If you want to make a richer version, spread the dough with sweetened cocoa or ground walnuts instead of the creamed butter

Rose cake

and sugar, but be careful with the cocoa filling, because if any leaks out on to the bottom of the tin, the dough will stick and it will be very difficult to get the cake out in one piece.

Notes

CAKES WITHOUT FILLING

Marigold cake (a basic recipe)

150 g	plain flour	5 oz
50 g	potato flour or ground rice	2 oz
4	eggs, separated	4
200 g	butter or margarine	7 oz
200 g	icing sugar	7 oz
	grated rind of 1 orange or lemon	
	salt	
200 g	candied or glacé cherries or sour cherries	7 oz
100 ml	single cream, shipped	⅕ pt
	a few fresh cherries	

Cream the butter and sugar until light and fluffy, then beat in the egg yolks one by one. Fold in the flour and ground rice a little at a time. Add the grated orange or lemon rind, a pinch of salt, the glacé cherries and lastly the stiffly beaten egg whites. Grease a round cake tin, then dust with flour. Smooth in the cake mixture and bake in a preheated oven (180° C/350° F/Gas 4) for approximately 35 minutes.
Leave to cool in the tin, then turn out on to a plate and decorate the top with a trellis pattern or rose pattern of whipped cream and the fresh cherries. (Use bottled cherries if fresh are not available.)
Note: Instead of glacé fruit you can sandwich the cake with any cream you like.

Golden cake (made with pumpkin)

1 kg	pumpkin	2¼ lb
50 g	butter or margarine	2 oz
3	eggs, separated	3
	rind of ½ lemon	
50 g	breadcrumbs	2 oz
150 g	mixed candied fruit	5 oz
100 ml	rum	⅕ pt
3 tbs	milk	3 tbs
50 g	castor sugar	2 oz
	salt	

Put the candied fruit in a bowl with the rum and leave to soak. Peel the pumpkin with a sharp knife and then grate using a medium-sized grater. Place in a saucepan with the milk and the lemon rind cut into strips. Cook until it turns to a pulp. Put aside until lukewarm, then add the sugar, butter, the drained and diced candied fruit, the breadcrumbs, egg yolks and a pinch of salt. Lastly fold in the stiffly beaten egg whites, whisked with a tiny pinch of salt. Grease a cake tin and dust with flour. Spoon the mixture into the tin and bake for approximately 50 minutes in an oven preheated to 160–180° C/325–350° F/Gas 3–4 until the top begins to crack. Test with a meat skewer. Leave to cool in the cake tin. Serve cold or lukewarm.

Potato cake

(for 6–8 people)

800 g	potatoes	2 lb
150 g	icing sugar	5 oz
4	eggs, separated	4
80 g	blanched almonds	3 oz
	cinnamon	
2 tsp	butter	2 tsp
	breadcrumbs	
	salt	
	apricot jam	

Wash the potatoes and cook in their skins. Peel while still hot and mash. Beat the almonds and sugar in a mortar until thick and creamy. (On first hearing this might sound rather strange, but the truth is that the sugar soon absorbs all the almond oil.) This could also be done in an electric grinder. Add the almonds to the mashed potatoes. Beat in the egg yolks one at a time, a pinch of salt, 2 pinches of cinnamon and, finally, the stiffly beaten egg whites. Grease a cake tin and sprinkle with breadcrumbs. Spoon in the cake mixture and bake for about 40 minutes in an oven preheated to 180° C/350° F/Gas 4. Serve still slightly warm with hot jam (apricot jam is the best).
Note: This is a traditional "Grandmother's" cake and brings back many happy childhood memories. It is extremely easy to make and takes very little time. A simple, not-very-filling soup could be served beforehand.

Carrot cake

(for 6–8 people)

200 g	carrots	7 oz
150 g	icing sugar	5 oz
150 g	blanched almonds	5 oz
100 g	ground rice or potato flour	4 oz
4	eggs, separated	4
	grated rind of 1 lemon	
	salt	
2 tsp	butter	2 tsp
	vanilla icing sugar (see p. 60)	

Wash and scrape the carrots. Dry thoroughly then grate finely. Split the almonds into halves and chop into thin shreds. Cream the butter and icing sugar until thick and fluffy. Add the carrots and almonds. Fold in the flour a little at a time and then add the grated lemon rind and a pinch of salt. Finally, blend in the stiffly beaten egg whites. Grease a round cake tin and dust with flour. Spoon in the mixture and bake for about 35 minutes in a preheated oven (180° C/350° F/Gas 4). Turn out on to a plate when cool and dust with vanilla sugar.
Note: If you have a little free time and feel like doing something special for this otherwise very simple cake, you could make some decorative paper patterns, very similar to those children make. With a little icing sugar and the use of these paper patterns, you can make the top of the cake very attractive.
To do this, simply place the cake tin base on a piece of paper. Draw round the base and cut out. Fold the paper circle in half, then in half again and so on, depending on the size of the pattern you wish to make. Then draw the outline of whatever shape you like—hearts, squares, circles, etc. Carefully cut out the shape with some sharp scissors. Unfold the paper, lay it on top of the cake and sprinkle icing sugar over the paper. Lift up the paper pattern carefully to reveal a lovely decoration on top of the cake. You can make several paper patterns like this, which you can put away and use again.

Swiss rice cake

Swiss rice cake

200 g	cooked rice	7 oz
150 g	deep-frozen puff pastry	5 oz
250 ml	single cream	½pt
90 g	icing sugar	3½ oz
100 g	apricots and peaches	4 oz
4	eggs, separated	4
2 tsp	butter	2 tsp
3 tbs	aromatic liqueur	3 tbs

Grease a deep oblong cake tin, one which will hold about 1 litre (2 pints) of liquid. Thaw the puff pastry and cut off one-third for the lid. Roll out the larger part and line the tin so that the pastry overlaps by approximately 2–3 cm (1–1¼ in).
Put the cold, cooked rice in a large bowl, then add the cream, sugar, 4 egg yolks, the drained and diced fruit and the liqueur. Mix thoroughly together. Whisk the egg whites with a pinch of salt until stiff and fold gently into the mixture. Spoon into the tin and fold the overlapping pastry over the top. Roll out the remaining pastry to fit the tin and press the edges lightly together. Bake in a preheated oven (180° C/350° F/Gas 4) for approximately 30 minutes. If the pastry is beginning to brown too much, cover with kitchen foil or greaseproof paper.
The top can be covered with chocolate glaze or apricot jam mixed with a little liqueur.

Aniseed chestnut cake

Aniseed chestnut cake

(for 8–10 people)

500 g	chestnuts	1¼ lb
200 g	icing sugar	7 oz
4	eggs, separated	4
100 g	butter or margarine	4 oz
80 g	blanched almonds	3 oz
1 tbs	aniseeds	1 tbs
	salt	
	a little vanilla sugar (see p. 60)	

Make a small cut on the flat side of each chestnut. Put into a pan with boiling water and blanch for a few minutes. Remove from pan and carefully peel off the two layers of skin. Put in another pan with a pinch of salt, a little water and the aniseeds in a tea infuser. Bring to the boil, cover with a lid and simmer until the chestnuts are tender. Drain the chestnuts and rub them through a hair sieve. Cream the butter and sugar until light and fluffy, then beat in the egg yolks one by one, the chestnuts, coarsely chopped almonds and lastly the stiffly beaten egg whites. Turn into a greased, floured cake tin and bake in a preheated oven (180°C/350° F/Gas 4) for about 35 minutes. (Do not open the oven door for the first 25 minutes.) Leave the cake in the tin to cool. Turn out on to a plate and dust the top with vanilla icing sugar.
This is a particularly delicious cake due to the unusual combination of aniseed and chestnut.

Lemon rice cake

250 g	cooked rice	9 oz
200 g	rich flan pastry (see p. 48)	7 oz
4	eggs, separated	4
	juice of 4 lemons	
90 g	icing sugar	3½ oz
40 g	honey	1½ oz
250 ml	single cream	½ pt
100 g	cream cheese	4 oz
60 g	nuts and dried fruit: walnuts, hazelnuts, sultanas, dates, figs	2½oz
2 tsp	butter	2 tsp

Grease an oblong cake tin. Put the dates, figs and sultanas into a small bowl with a little lukewarm water or rum and leave to soak. Place the cold cooked rice in a large bowl and add the sugar, egg yolks, strained lemon juice, cream cheese and the cream in which the honey has been dissolved.

Chop the drained fruit and nuts and add to the mixture. Mix very thoroughly. Finally fold in the stiffly beaten egg whites with a spoon.

Roll out the rich flan pastry and line the tin, allowing a big enough overlap so that the pastry can be folded over the top and meets in the middle. Spoon in the rice mixture, fold the pastry over the top, cover with kitchen foil or greaseproof paper and bake in a preheated oven (180° C/350° F/Gas 4) for approximately 30 minutes.

Leave to cool in the tin. Turn out on to an oblong dish and serve sliced (1½ cm–½–¾ in thick) with wine sauce (see p. 63) or vanilla cream.

Almond semolina cake

250 g	semolina	9 oz
1 litre	milk	2 pt
150 g	castor sugar	5 oz
4	eggs, separated	4
80 g	blanched almonds	3 oz
2–3	small pieces of lemon rind	2–3
50 g	butter	2 oz
	salt	
	breadcrumbs	
	sour cherry, apricot, raspberry or red currant jam	

Bring the milk to the boil in a pan with a pinch of salt and the pieces of lemon rind. Sprinkle in the semolina and, stirring constantly, cook until soft (approximately 10–15 minutes). Remove the lemon rind, add the ground almonds, the sugar and 30 g (1 oz) of the butter and put aside to cool until lukewarm. (Stir from time to time to prevent a skin from forming on the top.) Beat in the egg yolks one at a time, then add the stiffly beaten egg whites. Grease a cake tin and sprinkle with breadcrumbs. Spoon in the cake mixture.

Bake in a preheated oven (180° C/350° F/Gas 4) for approximately 40 minutes. (Do not open the oven door for 20 minutes, otherwise the cake will collapse.)

Serve warm with jam.

This cake is quick and inexpensive and will be a favourite with children.

Swedish almond cake

(for 6–8 people)

250 g	plain flour	9 oz
250 g	butter or margarine	9 oz
250 g	castor sugar	9 oz
60 g	blanched almonds	2½ oz
50 g	red currant jelly	2 oz
3	eggs	3
20 g	vanilla sugar (see p. 60)	¾ oz

Cream the butter and sugar until light and fluffy. Add the eggs one at a time. Fold in the flour gradually and lastly the vanilla sugar. Grease a round or square cake tin and dust with flour. Spoon in the mixture, spread the red currant jelly on top and sprinkle with the ground or grated almonds. Bake in a preheated oven (180° C/350° F/Gas 4) for approximately 35 minutes. Test with a meat skewer. If it comes out clean the cake is done. Do not open the oven door for the first 20 minutes. Leave to cool in the tin. Turn out on to a plate and slice.

Pistachio (or hazelnut) chocolate cake

200 g	icing sugar	7 oz
100 g	butter or margarine	4 oz
3 tbs	milk	3 tbs
2	eggs, separated	2
200 g	plain flour	7 oz
2 tsp	baking powder	2 tsp

Swedish almond cake

2 tsp	cocoa	2 tsp
100 g	pistachio or hazelnuts	4 oz
100 g	sultanas	4 oz
3 tbs	rum	3 tbs
	vanilla icing sugar (see p. 60)	

Place the sultanas in a small bowl with the rum and leave to soak. Cream the butter and sugar until light and fluffy. Beat in the egg yolks one at a time. Gradually add the milk and flour, then the baking powder, cocoa, and the roughly chopped nuts. Drain the sultanas, turn in a little flour and add to the mixture. Mix thoroughly. Finally, fold in the stiffly beaten egg whites. Grease a round cake tin and dust with flour. Spoon in the cake mixture and bake in a preheated oven (180° C/350° F/Gas 4) for approximately 40 minutes.
Cool in the tin, turn out and dust with vanilla icing sugar.

Chocolate cake with hazelnut kisses

(for 6–8 people)

200 g	deep-frozen flaky pastry	7 oz
150 g	hazelnut or almond kisses	5 oz
150 ml	milk	¼ pt
80 g	plain chocolate	3 oz
80 g	castor sugar	3 oz
2	eggs	2
100 ml	cocoa liqueur	⅕ pt
20 g	vanilla sugar (see p. 60)	¾ oz
	a little icing sugar flour	

Roll out the flaky pastry on a floured surface in a circle, to line a cake tin 22–25 cm (8½–10 in) in diameter and 3–4 cm (1¼–1¾ in) deep. Grease the

Pistachio (or hazelnut) chocolate cake

Chocolate cake with hazelnut kisses

tin and dust with flour then line it with the pastry. Prick the bottom with a fork. Beat one of the eggs in a small bowl and brush the bottom and sides of the pastry with it. Arrange the hazelnut kisses closely together on the pastry and sprinkle with the liqueur. Beat the other egg and any remaining beaten egg with the sugar and vanilla sugar until thick and fluffy. Add the milk in a thin stream, beating vigorously. Cut the chocolate into small pieces, sprinkle over the hazelnut kisses, then pour over the egg mixture.

Bake in a preheated oven (190–200° C/375–400° F/ Gas 5–6) for about 40 minutes. Leave to cool in the tin, turn out on to a plate. Place a small plate in the middle of the cake. Sprinkle the edge of the cake with icing sugar, then remove the plate. Serve sliced like an ordinary cake. It is extremely quick to prepare and is bound to be a success every time. Make sure, however, that the cake is cooked right through.

Hazelnut chocolate cake

(for 8 people)

300 g	deep-frozen flaky pastry	11 oz
150 g	castor sugar	5 oz
100 ml	milk	1/5 pt
100 g	hazelnuts	4 oz
90 g	plain chocolate	3 1/2 oz
3	eggs	3
2	ratafia biscuits	2
20 g	vanilla sugar (see p. 60)	3/4 oz
200 ml	double whipping cream	2/5 pt
2–3	hazelnut kisses	2–3
	a little icing sugar	
10 g	butter, for greasing	2 tsp
	salt	

Roll out the flaky pastry into a circle, big enough to line a sandwich cake tin 25–28 cm (10–11 in) in diameter. Whisk the eggs with the sugar, vanilla sugar and a pinch of salt until thick and fluffy. Then gradually beat in the milk, the melted chocolate and finally the peeled, slightly toasted and coarsely chopped hazelnuts. Mix thoroughly together. (This should only take a few minutes with an electric beater.) Line a greased tin with the pastry, prick with a fork, sprinkle with the crushed ratafia biscuits and spoon in the mixture. Bake in a preheated oven (180° C/ 350° F/Gas 4) for approximately 45 minutes. Make sure that the cake is cooked right through. Turn out on to a wire rack and leave to cool. When it is cold put on a plate, place a small plate or a paper circle in the middle of the cake. Sprinkle the edges of the cake with icing sugar and remove the paper. Whip the cream until thick, and pipe roses round the edge of the cake and one in the middle. Sprinkle the "cream roses" with the crushed hazelnut kisses and serve.

It looks spectacular and tastes very good.

Plain hazelnut cake

6	eggs, separated	6
150 g	plain flour	5 oz
150 g	peeled hazelnuts	5 oz
200 g	castor sugar	7 oz

Toast the hazelnuts in a pan for a few minutes. Place in a clean cloth, rub off the skins and grind the nuts. Beat the sugar and egg yolks in a large bowl until thick and fluffy. Add the ground hazelnuts, the flour a little at a time, a pinch of salt and finally the stiffly beaten egg whites. Grease a cake tin and dust with flour. Spoon in the mixture and bake in a preheated oven (180° C/350° F/Gas 4) for about 35 minutes. Do not open the oven door for the first 20 minutes, otherwise the cake will collapse.

Leave to cool in the tin before turning out on to a plate. This cake might not look spectacular but the taste is heavenly.

Greek cake

(for 6–8 people)

250 g	plain flour	9 oz
150 g	castor sugar	5 oz
50 g	sultanas	2 oz
50 g	butter or margarine	2 oz
25 g	pistachio nuts or almonds	1 oz
2	eggs, separated	2
100 ml	milk	1/5 pt
3 tbs	brandy	3 tbs
2 heaped tsp	baking powder	2 heaped tsp
	grated rind of 1 lemon	
	vanilla icing sugar (see p. 60)	

Soak the sultanas in a bowl with a little lukewarm water and put aside. Place the flour and sugar in a large bowl, make a well in the centre and gradually beat in the milk, the cooled, melted butter and the egg yolks. Mix thoroughly. Then add the brandy, grated lemon rind, the ground pistachio nuts or almonds and the baking powder. Drain the sultanas, turn in flour and add to the mixture. Finally fold in the stiffly beaten egg whites with a spoon as lightly as possible. Grease a round cake tin and dust with flour. Spoon in the mixture and bake in a preheated oven (200° C/400° F/Gas 6) for approximately 35 minutes. Leave to cool in the tin. Turn out and dust with vanilla icing sugar.

Sacher cake

(for 6–8 people)

150 g	plain flour	5 oz
150 g	butter	5 oz
150 g	plain chocolate	5 oz
6	eggs, separated	6
150 g	icing sugar	5 oz
	salt	
	for the glaze	
200 g	castor sugar	7 oz
100 g	plain chocolate	4 oz
50 g	apricot jam	2 oz

Grate the chocolate into a small pan with 2 tablespoons of water and melt over a low heat or in a double boiler. Melt the butter in a separate pan, then add to the chocolate. Cream the egg yolks and icing sugar until thick and fluffy. Gradually add to the chocolate, beating all the time. Whisk the egg whites with a pinch of salt until stiff. Gradually fold into the mixture alternating with the flour. Do this as lightly as possible so that the egg whites do not lose their stiffness.

Grease a round cake tin 22–25 cm (8¾—10 in) in diameter and dust with flour. Spoon in the mixture and bake in a preheated oven (220° C/400° F/ Gas 6) for about 35 minutes. Do not open the oven door for the first 25 minutes, otherwise the cake will collapse.

Leave in the cake tin for a few minutes, then turn out on to a wire rack. Leave to cool.

To prepare the glaze put the sugar and about 3 tablespoons of water into a pan and warm over a low heat, stirring all the time. Add the grated chocolate and leave over the heat for a few minutes stirring constantly. Spread the top of the cake with the apricot jam, then cover the top and the sides with the glaze. Place in a cool, switched-off oven for a minute or two, so that the glaze becomes smooth and beautifully shiny.

Note: This is perhaps the most famous Viennese cake. The recipe has been protected by special copyright for nearly two hundred years and it is thanks to one member of the Sacher dynasty of cooks, confectioners and hoteliers in Vienna that the gourmets of the world today can enjoy it. To this day it is still sold in its original packing—the characteristic, square wooden with copper fastener, in which the cake stays fresh for weeks.

Notes

_____
_____
_____
_____
_____
_____
_____
_____
_____
_____
_____
_____
_____
_____
_____
_____
_____
_____
_____
_____
_____
_____
_____
_____
_____
_____
_____
_____
_____

CAKES WITH A FILLING

Moldavian cheese cake

(for 6–8 people)

200 g	flan pastry (see p. 38)	7 oz
½	bought or homemade sandwich cake	½
	for the cream	
400 g	curd cheese	14 oz
4	egg yolks	4
100 g	icing sugar	4 oz
20 g	vanilla sugar (see p. 60)	¾ oz
	grated rind of 1 lemon	
10 g	gelatine	1 sachet
3 tbs	milk	3 tbs
300 ml	double cream for whipping	½ pt
50–60 g	apricot jam	2–2½ oz
200 g	pineapple or apricots	7 oz
	vanilla icing sugar	

If you use a ready made sandwich cake, this sweet can be prepared in next to no time. Use deep-frozen flan pastry or prepare your own.

Moldavian cheese cake

Place the pastry dough on a floured surface and roll into a circle the same size as the sandwich cake. Grease a shallow baking tray or flan tin and dust with flour. Bake blind in a preheated oven (180° C/350° F/Gas 4) for 15 minutes until light golden brown. Trim the edges of the pastry if necessary, so that it is exactly the same size as the sandwich cake and the tin you are going to use. Put the pastry in the bottom of the tin. Heat half the apricot jam and spread over the pastry. Slice the sandwich cake into two layers, put half aside for use on another occasion. Then divide the cake in half again. Place one layer on top of the pastry. Sprinkle with the drained and diced canned fruit. Rub the curd cheese through a hair sieve and add the sugar, vanilla sugar, egg yolks and lemon rind. Dissolve the gelatine in the milk and add to the mixture.

Lastly fold in the stiff whipped cream and the remaining jam. Spoon into the tin and cover with the second layer of cake. Cover with kitchen foil and leave to chill in the refrigerator for 2–3 hours. Before serving slip on to a serving plate and dust with vanilla icing sugar and slice into wedges. It is very light and simply delicious. It can be made with a combination of any bottled fruit you like.

Rich Hungarian cheese cake

(for 6–8 people)

	for the filling	
400 g	curd cheese	1 lb
100 g	apricot jam	4 oz
80 g	castor sugar	3 oz
50 g	hazelnut or almond kisses	2 oz
50 g	sultanas	2 oz
50 g	ground walnuts	2 oz
50 g	ground almonds or hazelnuts	2 oz
2	eggs, separated	2
1	egg white	1
	for the rich flan pastry	
180 g	plain flour	5 oz
120 g	butter or margarine	4½
70 g	castor sugar	3 oz
1	egg yolk	1
20 g	vanilla sugar (see p. 60)	¾ oz
	salt	

Put the sultanas in a small bowl with a little water and leave to soak. Grease a fluted, fireproof flan dish and dust with flour. To make the pastry put the flour into a bowl, rub in the butter, then add the sugar, vanilla sugar, the egg yolk and a pinch of salt. Mix well, roll and line the flan dish.

To make the filling rub the curd cheese through a hair sieve. Add the sugar, 2 egg yolks, the ground almonds or hazelnuts, the ground walnuts and the drained sultanas. Mix thoroughly. Finally lightly fold in the 3 stiffly beaten egg whites. Crumble the hazelnut or almond kisses and sprinkle over the pastry. Spoon in the cheese mixture and bake in a preheated oven (200° C/400° F/Gas 6) for approximately 40 minutes until deep golden brown. Leave to cool in the flan dish, then using two spatulas carefully lift the cake out and place it on a plate. Add a little water or liqueur to the apricot jam and spread it over the cake. Serve cold.

Note: This cake is at its best if prepared 4–5 hours before you plan to eat it, or even the day before.

Curd cheese cake

(for 6–8 people)

300 g	curd cheese	11 oz
300 g	plain flour	11 oz
300 g	icing sugar	11 oz
3	eggs	3
20 g	baking powder	2 tsp
	a little milk, salt	
	grated rind of 1 lemon	
	vanilla icing sugar (see p. 60)	

Mix the sugar and curd cheese together thoroughly, then beat in the eggs one at a time until the mixture is thick and fluffy. Gradually fold in the flour and lastly the baking powder dissolved in a little milk, the grated lemon rind and a pinch of salt. Grease a round cake tin and dust with flour. Spoon in the cake mixture and bake in a preheated oven (180° C/350° F/Gas 4) for approximately 35 minutes. Leave to cool in the tin then turn out and sprinkle generously with vanilla icing sugar. It is delicious on its own but can be served with hot jam sauce (jam heated and mixed with a little aromatic liqueur).

Sour-cherry cream cake

(for 6–8 people)

1	round chocolate sandwich cake (if you are making your own, see p. 77)	1

400 ml	single cream	¾ pt
50 g	castor sugar	2 oz
100 g	plain chocolate	4 oz
100 g	sour-cherries in rum	4 oz
100 ml	rum-flavoured sour-cherry juice	⅕ pt

To make sour cherries in rum soak cherries in water then use 400 g (14 oz) castor sugar to each kilo (2 lb) of fruit and 200 ml (⅖ pt) or more of rum. Put layers of cherries, then sugar and rum in a jar. Shake to dissolve the sugar. Do not screw on the top until the cherries have risen to the top.
Note: The day before you plan to make the cake put the cream into a pan with the sugar and bring to the boil. Break the chocolate into the pan and stir well until it has melted. Put aside to cool, then keep in the refrigerator overnight. Slice the chocolate cake into three equal layers. Whisk the chilled chocolate cream until thick (you will find that it will last longer and be much thicker if it is boiled the previous day). When whipped return to the coldest part of the refrigerator. Stone and drain the cherries. Place the bottom layer of the cake on

a circular plate. Sprinkle with a little of the rum and cherry juice followed by a layer of chocolate cream and then some of the cherries. Put the second layer of cake on top and repeat this process. Make sure that you leave enough chocolate cream to coat the sides as well as the top of the cake and also to pipe some decorative roses. You can put a cherry in the centre of each "cream rose" if you wish.

It is quick, simple and bound to be a success.
Note: According to the traditional recipes this should have a chocolate glaze on the top, but I think it is too rich like that.

Rich chocolate cake

(for 6–8 people)

400 ml	whipping cream	¾ pt
200 g	castor sugar	7 oz
200 g	plain chocolate	7 oz
150 ml	milk	¼ pt

Sour-cherry cream cake

115 g	plain flour	4½ oz
75 g	dark vermicelli	3 oz
50 g	blanched almonds	2 oz
50 g	rice or potato flour	2 oz
20 g	cocoa	¾ oz
5	eggs	5
20 g	vanilla sugar (see p. 60)	¾ oz
20 g	baking powder	2 tsp
	salt	

Grease a round cake tin appr. 23 cm (9 in) in diameter and dust with flour. Cream 3 eggs and 150 g (5 oz) of the sugar in a large bowl until thick and fluffy. In a separate bowl mix together 100 g (4 oz) of the flour, the ground rice or potato flour, the cocoa, the baking powder and vanilla sugar. Gradually add to the egg mixture with a spoon making vertical up-and-down movements rather than circular ones. Melt 60 g (2½ oz) of the chocolate in a small bowl over boiling water. Leave it to cool a little then add to the mixture. Spoon into the cake tin and bake in a preheated oven (180° C/350° F/Gas 4) for approximately 30 minutes. Turn out on to a wire rack when lukewarm. *Meanwhile prepare the cream:* Beat the 2 remaining egg yolks with the rest of the flour and sugar, and a pinch of salt until smooth. Add the milk a little at a time, pour into a pan and cook over a low heat or over a pan of boiling water stirring all the time until it almost reaches boiling point. (Do not let it boil.) Melt the remaining chocolate and stir into the cream. Blend thoroughly together then put aside to cool. Whisk the cream until stiff then fold very lightly into the cold cream. Split the cake into 3 and sandwich together with the cream, making sure that you leave enough to spread a thin layer on the sides and to decorate the top with rosettes. Sprinkle the vermicelli all over the cake and pipe small rosettes round the top edge of the cake. Pipe some in the middle too. Decorate the rest of the top with shredded almonds. Chill for 4–5 hours before eating. This cake is really delicious and very spectacular. It should only be prepared for special occasions.

Sultana-cream sandwich

(for 6–8 people)

1	bought sandwich cake weighing 500 g (1¼ lb) or a water sponge cake made with 6 eggs (see p. 61)	1

Cake diplomatique

3 tbs	dark rum	3 tbs
100 g	sultanas	4 oz
100 ml	milk	⅕ pt
150 g	butter or margarine	5 oz
300 g	icing sugar	11 oz
3	eggs, separated	3

Put the sultanas in a bowl with water to soak. Split the cake into 3. Crumble the bottom layer into a bowl and pour over the rum and milk. Add the drained sultanas. Cream the butter, 100 g (4 oz) of the icing sugar and the egg yolks until thick and fluffy. Add the crumbled cake mixture and beat until smooth. Sandwich the other 2 layers of cake with the cream, spreading some on top as well. Whisk the 3 egg whites and the rest of the sugar (220 g–7 oz) over a pan of boiling water until stiff and glossy. Spread on top of the cake, smoothing the surface with a wet knife.

Note: The egg white, because it has been whisked over steam and so partially "cooked", will not separate and will stay looking very attractive.

Cake diplomatique

200 g	puff pastry	7 oz
500 ml	vanilla cream made with milk (see p.62)	1 pt
200 g	plain chocolate	7 oz

| 100 ml | dark rum | 1/5 pt |
| 20 | sponge fingers | 20 |

Roll out the puff pastry into a rectangle approximately 20 cm (8 in) by 30–35 cm (12–13 ¾ in). Place on a floured tin and bake in a preheated oven (180° C/350° F/Gas 4) for about 20 minutes until light golden brown. Leave to cool then remove from the tin and trim the edge.

Meanwhile prepare the vanilla cream and chill. Place the pastry in an oblong dish. Spread with half the cream. Place a row of sponge fingers on top. Sprinkle with half the rum, followed by another row of sponge fingers, the rest of the rum and the remaining cream. Sprinkle the top generously with coarsely grated chocolate and chill in the refrigerator for 2–3 hours. The cake will be even better if prepared the night before.

Note: This is a relatively quick cake to prepare. It tastes very good and looks spectacular. If you want a richer sweet, it can be served with whipped cream.

Tipsy star gateau

(for 6–8 people)

1	round chocolate sandwich cake, bought ready made or prepared with 6 eggs (see p. 60)	1
300 ml	whipping cream	1/2 pt
200 g	apricot jam	7 oz
150 ml	milk	5 fl oz
50 g	castor sugar	2 oz
25 g	icing sugar	1 oz
50 g	blanched hazelnuts	2 oz
1	egg yolk	1
	grated rind of 1 lemon, salt	
1½ tbs	almond liqueur	1½ tbs
1½ tbs	orange liqueur	1½ tbs
1½ tbs	maraschino liqueur	1½ tbs
1 tbs	flour	1 tbs
	chocolate or other flavoured drops for decoration	

First of all cut out an eight-pointed paper star to fit the top of the cake. Place on cake and using a sharp pointed knife carefully cut the cake into the star shape. Then slice into 4 layers. Beat the egg yolk, castor sugar and flour until thick. Add a pinch of salt and the grated lemon rind. Pour into a pan and gradually beat in the milk. Place over a low heat and bring nearly to the boil, stirring all the time. Remove from the heat and stir in the orange liqueur. Put aside to cool, stirring occa-

sionally to prevent a skin from forming on the top. Whip the cream until stiff, add the icing sugar, and put 4–5 tablespoonfuls aside for decoration. Place the bottom layer of the cake on a plate and sprinkle with half the almond liqueur. Spread with a little of the apricot jam (remove any apricot pieces, or rub through a sieve), followed by some of the cold cooked cream and then whipped cream. Place the second layer of cake on top. Sprinkle with half the maraschino liqueur and the jam and cream. Do the same with the third and fourth layer, putting the rest of the almond liqueur on the third and the maraschino liqueur on the top. Chop the peeled hazelnuts coarsely and sprinkle over the top of the cake. Decorate with piped cream rosettes and place a chocolate drop in the middle of each rosette.

Keep chilled until ready to use. It looks wonderful and tastes absolutely delicious.

Quick as a wink coffee cake

(for 6–8 people)

400 g	sponge fingers	14 oz
200 ml	strong black coffee or instant coffee made with 2 heaped tbs. powder	2/5 pt
4	eggs, separated	4
80 g	icing sugar	3 oz
250 ml	milk	1/2 pt
250 ml	whipping cream	1/2 pt
3–6 tbs	dark rum	3–6 tbs

Beat the egg yolks and sugar until thick and fluffy. Place over a pan of boiling water and gradually add the milk stirring all the time until it thickens enough to cover the back of a wooden spoon. Remove from the heat and add the coffee when it has cooled slightly. When it is quite cold fold in the whipped cream.

Sprinkle the sponge fingers with the rum. Arrange a row of sponge fingers on the bottom of a round or oval dish. Spread with cream, followed by another layer of sponge cake and so on until all the ingredients are used up. Put aside just enough cream to spread thinly over the top and sides of the cake.

Like most sweets that do not require cooking, it is advisable to prepare this the day before you plan to eat it.

It can be decorated with a few coffee beans or whipped cream rosettes.

It is very delicious and quick and simple to make.

Coffee cake

(for 6–8 people)

150 g	plain flour	5 oz
80 g	butter or margarine	3 oz
5	eggs, separated	5
150 g	icing sugar	5 oz
	salt	
	grated lemon rind	
	for the filling	
100 g	butter or margarine	4 oz
100 g	icing sugar	4 oz
100 ml	strong black coffee or	1/5 pt
2 tbs	instant coffee	2 tbs
3 tbs	brandy	3 tbs

Cream the butter and sugar until light and fluffy. Beat in the egg yolks one at a time. Gradually fold in the flour, and add a pinch of salt and the grated lemon rind. Mix thoroughly then lightly fold in the stiffly beaten egg whites. Grease a round cake tin and dust with flour. Spoon in the cake mixture and bake in a preheated oven (180° C/350° F/Gas 4) for approximately 35 minutes. (Do not open the oven door for the first 20–25 minutes, otherwise the cake will collapse.) Leave to cool in the tin. *Meanwhile prepare the cream:* Cream the butter and sugar until light and fluffy, add the coffee and mix thoroughly. Split the cake in two. Sprinkle the brandy on the cut side of each layer. Sandwich together with the cream, leaving enough to spread a thin layer on the top and sides. Decorate with a few coffee beans and chill in the refrigerator for a few hours.

Note: If you are preparing this dessert with a ready-made shop cake, it is best to buy a chocolate flavoured one.

Brazilian coffee cake

(for 8–10 people)

300 g	plain flour	11 oz
180 g	icing sugar	6 oz
3	eggs	3
100 g	butter or margarine	4 oz
100 ml	strong coffee or	1/5 pt
2 tbs	instant coffee	2 tbs
20 g	baking powder	2 tbs
	for the filling	
400 g	plain chocolate	14 oz
80 g	butter	3 oz
100 ml	dark rum	1/5 pt

Cream the butter and icing sugar until light and fluffy. Beat in the eggs one at a time, then the coffee. Gradually fold in the flour and baking powder. Mix thoroughly. Grease a round cake tin and dust with flour. Spoon in the cake mixture and bake in a preheated oven (180° C/350° F/Gas 4) for approximately 35 minutes. Leave to cool in the tin.

Meanwhile, break the chocolate into a bowl and melt it over boiling water, adding 1–2 tablespoons water. When it has cooled slightly add the butter and rum. Beat until fluffy. Slice the cold cake into 2 layers. Spread the bottom half with half the filling and place the top in position, pressing the 2 halves lightly together. Spread cream on the top and sides of the cake and chill for a few hours in the refrigerator.

This is a very rich cake so it should be cut into thin slices. Serve with whipped cream flavoured with a little vanilla sugar (see p.60).

Coffee cake

Brazilian coffee cake

round tin (about 22 cm— 8½ in in diameter) and dust with flour. Spoon in the cake mixture and bake in a preheated oven (180° C/350° F/Gas 4) for approximately 40 minutes. Leave to cool in the tin.

In the meantime prepare the cream: Put the milk, castor and vanilla sugar in a pan and warm until the sugar dissolves. Melt half the butter in a large pan. Remove from the heat and beat in the flour and egg yolk. Blend in the warm milk a little at a time. Simmer over a very low heat or place over a pan of boiling water. Cook until it thickens, stirring all the time. Put aside to cool.

Cream the remaining butter with the icing sugar until light and fluffy, then beat in the cold cream a spoonful at a time. Divide the cake in half. Sprinkle both layers with the rum and sandwich together with the cream. Spread the sides and top of the cake with the apricot jam, then cover evenly with coffee glaze. Decorate the top with a few hazelnuts or sliced candied fruit.

Note: Chocolate glaze can be used instead of coffee if preferred, or alternatively it can be topped with whipped cream and bottled fruit.

Trudy's hazelnut cake

(for 6–8 people)

150 g	plain flour	5 oz
150 g	castor sugar	5 oz
75 g	blanched hazelnuts	3 oz
6	eggs	6
	grated rind of 1 lemon	
1 tsp	vanilla sugar (see p. 60)	1 tsp
	for the filling	
80 g	butter	3 oz
50 g	icing sugar	2 oz
25 g	plain flour	1 oz
1	egg yolk	1
½ tsp	vanilla sugar	½ tsp
200 ml	milk	⅖ pt
30 g	castor sugar	1 oz
1–2 tbs	dark rum	1–2 tbs
50–70 g	apricot jam	2–2¾ oz
	coffee glaze (see p. 80)	

Beat 4 whole eggs and 2 egg yolks with the sugar until thick and fluffy. Place the bowl over a pan of boiling water and continue beating until the mixture warms slightly. Remove from the heat and beat until it is quite cold. Then gradually add the flour, vanilla sugar, grated lemon rind and the diced or coarsely ground hazelnuts. Grease a

Frankfurt cake with praline

(for 6–8 people)

125 g	plain flour	4½ oz
100 g	cornflour	4 oz
130 g	butter or margarine	4½ oz
125 g	castor sugar	4½ oz
10 g	vanilla sugar (see p. 60)	1 tsp
20 g	baking powder	1 heaped tsp
4	eggs, separated	4
	grated rind of 1 lemon, salt	
	for the filling	
150 g	butter or margarine	5 oz
100 g	castor sugar	4 oz
150 g	icing sugar	5 oz
80 g	blanched almonds	3 oz
10 g	vanilla sugar	1 tsp
1	egg yolk	1
3 tbs	dark rum	3 tbs

To make the cake: Cream the butter and sugar until light and fluffy, then beat in the egg yolks one at a time. In a separate bowl mix together the 2 types of flour, the vanilla sugar and baking powder. Fold lightly into the egg mixture a little at a time, alternating with the stiffly beaten egg whites to which a pinch of salt has been added. Lastly add

Frankfurt cake with praline

Marinka's punch gateau

(for 6–8 people)

1	round sandwich cake	1
100 g	butter	4 oz
150 g	icing sugar	5 oz
1	egg	1
100 ml	milk	⅕ pt
3 tbs	dark rum	3 tbs
100 ml	strong black coffee	⅕ pt
2 tbs	cocoa	2 tbs
50 g	sultanas	2 oz
50 g	walnuts	2 oz
100 ml	whipping cream	⅕ pt

This is not a traditional punch cake, but in my opinion it tastes even nicer.

Put the sultanas in a small bowl with some water and leave to soak. You can buy a plain sandwich cake for this recipe or make your own using 6 eggs (see p. 60). Put the cake on a plate and cut a thin layer from the top, approximately 1 cm (½ in) thick and put carefully aside. Remove the inside of the cake, leaving the sides and bottom intact, again about 1 cm (½ in) thick. Sprinkle the cake "case" with the milk mixed with half the rum. Beat the egg and sugar until thick and fluffy. Add the coffee and cocoa. Pour into a small pan and heat over boiling water stirring all the time. (Do not let it boil.) Remove from the heat, beat in the butter, the crumbled inside of the cake, the remaining rum, the drained sultanas and coarsely chopped walnuts. Stuff the cake "case" while the filling is still warm. Cover with the top of the cake and chill.

Decorate with whipped cream and serve cut into wedges.

Note: The cake is even more delicious if prepared one day in advance so that it absorbs all the liquid. For a special occasion it can be covered with a pink glaze made with a little food colouring or cherry juice (see p. 80).

the grated lemon rind. Grease a fluted or plain ring mould and dust with flour. Spoon in the cake mixture and bake in a preheated oven (180° C/350° F/Gas 4) for approximately 30 minutes. (Do not open the oven door for the first 25 minutes.) Leave to cool in the tin then turn out on to a plate.

While the cake is baking prepare the cream: Cream the butter, vanilla sugar and icing sugar until light and fluffy. Then add the egg yolk and rum. Put the castor sugar in a small pan with 1–2 tablespoons of water. Heat gently and as soon as the sugar turns caramel coloured throw in the coarsely chopped almonds. Continue to cook until the almonds and sugar are golden brown. Spread on to a buttered baking tray, allowing a thickness of approximately 3 mm (⅛ in). When it is hard break into pieces, then, crush with a mortar and pestle. Divide the cake in half horizontally and sandwich together with half the cream. Cover the top and sides with the cram and sprinkle the praline on top.

Tipsy cake

120 g	castor sugar	4½ oz
100 g	plain flour	4 oz
4	eggs, separated	4
4 tbs	Scotch whisky	4 tbs

Marinka's punch gateau

	for the cream	
35 g	castor sugar	1½ oz
400 ml	milk	¾ pt
4 tbs	Scotch whisky	4 tbs
3	eggs	3
	salt	
	for the decoration	
100–200 ml	whipping cream	⅕–⅖ pt
	glacé cherries or other candied fruit	
	blanched almonds	

To prepare the cake: Cream the 4 egg yolks with the sugar until thick and fluffy. Gradually beat in the flour, 2 tablespoons of lukewarm water and the whisky. Lightly fold in the stiffly beaten egg whites. Grease a ring tin and dust with flour. Spoon in the cake mixture and bake in a preheated oven (180° C/350° F/Gas 4) for approximately 40 minutes. (Do not open the oven door for the first 25 minutes.) Leave the cake in the tin for a few minutes before turning it out on to a round dish. When cold sprinkle with a little whisky.

To prepare the cream: Beat the eggs, the sugar and a pinch of salt vigorously, then gradually add the milk. Place over a pan of boiling water and stir until it thickens. Add the whisky while the cream is still hot, then spread over the cake. Whisk the cream until thick. Pile in the middle of the cake and decorate with glacé cherries and lightly roasted whole almonds.

Serve warm.

Not only the taste but the look is intoxicating.

Gabriella's walnut gateau

(for 6–8 people)

110 g	plain flour	4 oz
40 g	ground walnuts	1½ oz
120 g	castor sugar	4½ oz
6	eggs, separated	6
3 tbs	dark rum	3 tbs
	for the cream	
300 ml	milk	½ pt
60 g	plain flour	2 oz
150 g	icing sugar	5 oz
200 g	ground walnuts	7 oz
200 g	butter or margarine	7 oz
10 g	vanilla sugar (see p. 60)	1 tsp
3 tbs	dark rum	3 tbs

8–10	walnut halves for decoration	8–10

Beat the egg yolks with 40 g (1½ oz) of the sugar until thick and fluffy. Beat the egg whites and the rest of the sugar until stiff then lightly fold into the egg yolks with a spoon, alternating with the flour, a little of the rum and ground walnuts. For the folding in process do not use an electric beater but a hand whisk or a perforated wooden or metal spoon. Grease a round cake tin and line the bottom with greaseproof paper. Pour in the cake mixture and bake in a preheated oven (180° C/350° F/Gas 4) for about 30 minutes until light golden brown. Test with a meat skewer.

Leave to cool in the tin, then divide into 3–5 layers and sandwich with the following *cream:* Put the flour into a bowl and gradually add the milk. Beat until smooth. Place over a pan of boiling water and heat until it thickens, stirring all the time. Put aside to cool.

Meanwhile cream the butter and icing sugar until light and fluffy. Add the ground walnuts, the rum and vanilla sugar. Add to the cooked cream and beat vigorously together. Sandwich the cake together, leaving enough for the top and sides. Decorate with the walnut halves. It is so delicious that it deserves to be served on your most attractive plate. The cake will taste even nicer if it is prepared one day in advance.

Napoleon's cake

(requires no cooking)

250 g	sponge fingers	9 oz
4–6	almond meringue kisses	4–6
200 g	butter	7 oz
6	egg yolks	6
200 g	icing sugar	7 oz
200–300 ml	milk	⅖–½ pt
3 tbs	dark rum	3 tbs
50 g	plain chocolate or dark vermicelli	2 oz
8–10	glacé cherries or sour cherries in rum (see p. 60)	8–10

Beat the egg yolks and 100 g (4 oz) of the icing sugar until thick and fluffy. In another bowl cream the rest of the sugar with the butter. Beat in the egg and sugar mixture, a spoonful at a time and half the rum. Beat vigorously. Pour the milk and the rest of the rum into a bowl. Dip each sponge finger into the liquid and shape into a circle, roughly 24 cm (9½ in) in diameter, on the bottom

Napoleon's cake

10 g	vanilla sugar (see p. 66)	1 heaped tsp
20 g	gelatine	¾ oz
1 packet	chocolate pudding powder	1 packet
500 ml	milk	1 pt
50 g	castor sugar	2 oz
	a little aromatic liqueur	

The day before preparing the cake, put the cream, icing sugar and vanilla sugar into a pan and heat up to boiling point. Remove, allow to cool then cover with a lid and keep in the refrigerator overnight. The following day dissolve the gelatine in about 3 tablespoons of water. Beat quickly into the cream and whisk until thick. Put a little of the cream aside for decoration. Make a thick chocolate pudding following the instructions on the packet and put aside until lukewarm. Slice the cakes horizontally into 2 or 3 layers depending on the thickness. Place a layer of the chocolate cake on a glass or porcelain serving plate. Spread some chocolate pudding on top, followed by some whipped cream. Press a layer of the plain sandwich cake lightly on top. Spread with the pudding and cream. Continue until all the ingredients are used up. Sprinkle the top with a little liqueur and decorate with the rest of the cream, making a trellis pattern or by piping rosettes. Chill for 2–3 hours in the refrigerator before serving. Use 2 cake slices when serving the cake to stop the layers from coming apart. This cake looks really spectacular and is quite filling. It is ideal for children's birthday parties or when you have a lot of guests. If you plan to prepare it for children, use jam diluted with a little water instead of liqueur.

This enormous cake does not take much effort to make and it will the children with much greater happiness than a cake from the baker's shop.

of a large round serving dish. (Break up one or two sponge fingers to make the edges of the circle as even as possible.) Spread some of the cream over the top, then sprinkle with a little crumbled almond meringue. Continue with layers of sponge fingers, cream and almond meringue, but make sure to place each layer of sponge fingers at right angles to the previous one, as this will make it very attractive when cut into slices. Finish with enough cream to cover the top and sides. Lastly sprinkle the top and sides with grated chocolate or vermicelli and decorate the edges and middle with the glacé cherries or cherries in rum. Chill for at least 5 hours so that the sponge fingers absorb some of the liquid and the cream hardens.

Note: The consistency of the cream when just prepared will be runny, but don't worry it will be beautifully hard by the time it appears on the table.

Hungarian Battenberg cake

(for 10–12 people)

1	plain sandwich cake	1
1	chocolate sponge cake (ready-made, or see p. 60)	1
400 ml	whipping cream	¾ pt
50 g	icing sugar	2 oz

Cake supreme

1	bought or homemade plain sandwich cake (see p. 60)	1
	for the filling	
150 g	butter or margarine	5 oz
100 g	icing sugar	4 oz
4	egg yolks	4
2 tbs	dark rum or raspberry syrup	2 tbs
	for the top	
5	egg yolks	5
120 g	castor sugar	4½ oz

40 g	vanilla sugar (see p. 60)	1½ oz
1 tsp	ground cinnamon	1 tsp
2 heaped tbs	cocoa	2 heaped tbs
250 ml	milk	½ pt
100 g	plain chocolate	4 oz
15 g	gelatine	½ oz
250 ml	whipping cream	½ pt
	a little rum	

This delicious cake has to be prepared in 2 stages. *To prepare the cream:* Cream together the butter and sugar until light and fluffy. Add the egg yolks one at a time, then the rum (if you are making the cake for children use raspberry syrup instead). Spread thinly on the cake and roll up tightly like a Swiss roll. Wrap in kitchen foil and chill in the refrigerator for a few hours, or preferably overnight.

To prepare the second stage: Beat the egg yolks, sugar, vanilla sugar, cinnamon and cocoa until thick and fluffy. Bring the milk to the boil, break the chocolate into the pan and stirring vigorously add to the egg yolk mixture. Place over a pan of boiling water and stir until thick. Dissolve the gelatine in a little water and add to the cream while still hot. Beat thoroughly together. Finally fold in the stiffly whipped cream. Cut the Swiss roll into slices about 1 cm (½ in) thick, and line the bottom and sides of a round bowl. Add half the cream and spread evenly over the cake. Add another layer of cake then the rest of the cream. (If there is any cake left over arrange on top.) Cover and chill in the refrigerator for 3–4 hours. Turn out on to a plain round serving plate just before serving. (If it is difficult to get it out of the bowl, place in hot water for a few seconds, taking care not to get water on to the cake.) Sprinkle with a few drops of rum.

Cake supreme

Russian cream cake

(for 6–8 people)

	for the cake	
5	eggs	5
100 g	castor sugar	4 oz
100 g	plain flour	4 oz
	for the cream	
300 ml	milk	½ pt
5	egg yolks	5
200 g	castor sugar	7 oz
½	vanilla pod	½
15 g	gelatine	½ oz
400 ml	whipping cream	¾ pt
	grated rind of ½ lemon	
100 g	sultanas	4 oz
100 g	mixed candied fruit	4 oz
150–200 ml	dark rum	¼–⅖ pt
200 ml	whipping cream	⅖ pt

Make a sandwich cake following the recipe on page 77. Divide the mixture into 4 or 5 cake tins before baking. Cut them while still hot if necessary to fit the cake tin you are using for this recipe. Then leave to cool.

To prepare the cream: Prepare a vanilla cream in the usual way with the milk, egg yolks, sugar, vanilla, and lemon rind (see p. 79) but without flour. Dissolve the gelatine in a little water and add to the cream while it is still hot. Leave to cool, then fold in the stiffly whipped cream.

If the sultanas and candied fruit are hard soak in a bowl with a little rum. The cake will be the nicest if the candied fruit includes some orange peel. Line the bottom and sides of the cake tin with greaseproof paper. Lay one of the sandwich cakes in the bottom, sprinkle with a little rum, spread with cream and put some of the drained sultanas and candied fruit on top. Repeat this process until you have used all the ingredients. Finish with a layer of cream.

Cover the cake and put in the refrigerator for a few hours. Lift the cake carefully out of the tin just before serving, and remove the greaseproof paper. Whip the cream and pipe rosettes on the tip and decorate with the cherries.

Variation: It can be made richer with the addition of drained cubes of pineapple (approximately 500 g–1¼ lb) which are arranged on the cream with the sultanas. Pineapple can be used instead of the candied fruit or with a smaller quantity. The orange peel should not be omitted.

KUGELHOPFS AND OTHER DELICACIES

Biscuit roll

(requires no cooking)

200 g	tea biscuits	7 oz
200 g	icing sugar	7 oz
2 tbs	apricot jam	2 tbs
1 tsp	cocoa	1 tsp
3 tbs	rum	3 tbs
	grated rind of 1 lemon	
50 g	butter	2 oz
	a little milk	

Grind or crush the biscuits, add 100 g (4 oz) of the sugar, the apricot jam, the cocoa, rum and lemon rind. Knead thoroughly together (add a little milk if the mixture is too dry). Place on a piece of kitchen foil and roll into a rectangle.

To make the filling cream the remaining icing sugar with the butter until light and fluffy. Spread thinly on to the rolled out biscuit mixture, then with the help of the kitchen foil roll tightly, like a Swiss roll. Wrap up in kitchen foil and put in the refrigerator for several hours. When serving dust with icing sugar and cut into thin slices. It is very quick to prepare and inexpensive. It will be a favourite at children's parties (in which case the rum should be replaced by rum flavouring).

Layered kugelhopf

(for 6–8 people)

1(700–750 g)	fluted kugelhopf or a round kolach	1 (1½ lb)
	for the filling	
500 ml	milk	1 pt
70 g	plain flour	3 oz
100 g	butter or margarine	4 oz
100 g	icing sugar	4 oz
	juice of 1 orange	
	grated rind of 2 oranges	
	juice of ½ lemon	
3 tbs	orange liqueur	3 tbs
	for the glaze	
200 g	plain chocolate for glazing	7 oz
100 g	butter	4 oz

Put the flour in a pan and gradually add the milk, beating it until quite smooth. Place over medium heat or over a pan of boiling water and cook for 10 minutes stirring all the time until it is thick. Stand the pan in cold water, stirring the cream occasionally to prevent a skin from forming on the top. In the meantime cream the butter and icing sugar until light and fluffy. Add the strained orange juice and lemon juice, the grated orange rind and orange liqueur. Lastly beat in the cold cream a spoonful at a time. Cut the kugelhopf into 7 thin horizontal slices. Push a tooth pick into the edge of each layer in a vertical line, so that they may be returned to their exact original position. Place the bottom layer of the kugelhopf (the largest one) on to a serving plate and spread with cream. Place the next layer on top (remember to line up the toothpicks) and spread with cream. Continue sandwiching all the layers until the kugelhopf is complete. Break the chocolate into small pieces. Put in a bowl with the butter and melt over a pan of boiling water. Spread an even layer of the glaze over the sides and top of the kugelhopf. Place in a cool, turned off oven for a few minutes to make the glaze smooth. Store in a cold place until ready to eat. The top can be decorated with piped cream rosettes or candied fruit.

This cake does not take very long to make. It looks very beautiful and would be ideal for special occasions.

Sultana and almond kugelhopf

150 g	plain flour	5 oz
50 g	ground rice	2 oz
100 g	butter or margarine	4 oz
100 g	icing sugar	4 oz
3	eggs, separated	3
20 g	baking powder	2 tsp
50 g	sultanas	2 oz
3 tbs	dark rum	3 tbs
50 g	blanched almonds	2 oz
50 g	mixed candied fruit	2 oz

Put the sultanas in a small bowl with the rum and leave to soak. Chop the almonds coarsely and dice the candied fruit. Cream the butter and icing sugar until light and fluffy. Beat in the egg yolks one at a time. Then gradually fold in the flour and ground rice and baking powder. Mix thoroughly. Drain the sultanas and dust with flour to stop them from sinking to the bottom of the cake. Shake off any excess flour in a sieve and add to the mixture. Fold in the almonds and candied fruit and finally the stiffly beaten egg whites. Grease a round fluted kugelhopf mould and dust

with flour. Spoon in the mixture, banging the bottom of the mould gently to get rid of bubbles of air. Bake in a preheated oven (180° C/350° F/ Gas 4) for approximately 35 minutes. Do not open the oven door for the first 25 minutes otherwise the cake will sink in the middle. Leave to cool in the mould, then turn out on to a serving plate and cut into wedges.

Rum kugelhopf (Rum Baba)

(for 6–8 people)

270 g	plain flour	10 oz
130 g	butter	4½ oz
20 g	icing sugar	¾ oz
10 g	yeast	½ oz
approx. 100 ml	milk	⅕pt
2	sugar lumps, if dried yeast is used	2
4	eggs	4
	salt	
70 g	sultanas	3 oz
	for the glaze	
70 g	castor sugar	3 oz
100 ml	dark rum	⅕pt

Cream the yeast in 1½ tablespoons of slightly warmed milk and add the sugar lumps. Add 70 g (3 oz) of the flour and mix to form a very soft dough. Add a little water if necessary. Shape into a ball, cover and leave in a warm place to rise for 20 minutes. Put the rest of the flour into a large bowl. Make a well in the centre and add the dough broken up into small pieces the size of a hazelnut, the eggs, a pinch of salt and approximately 3 tablespoons of lukewarm milk. Mix together and knead thoroughly, hanging the dough against the sides of the bowl until it is pliable and smooth. Finally work 1 tablespoon of flour into the butter and add to the dough a little at a time, kneading thoroughly. Shape into a ball and put in a clean bowl that has been dusted with flour. Cover with a kitchen cloth and leave in a warm place until it has doubled in size (this will take 1 to 1½ hours). Meanwhile put the sultanas in a small bowl with a little water and leave to soak. When the dough has risen dissolve the icing sugar in a teaspoon of warm water. Add to the dough. Drain the sultanas well, dust with flour and work into the dough. Grease a round fluted kugelhopf mould and dust with flour. Place the dough in the mould. It should come only half way up the sides. Cover once again with a kitchen cloth and leave in a warm place until the dough has risen almost to the rim of the mould. Bake in a preheated oven (200–220° C/400–425° F /Gas 6–7) for about 40 minutes. (Do not open the oven door for the first 30 minutes.) Test with a meat skewer by inserting it into the middle of the cake. If it comes out clean the cake is done. Leave to cool in the mould for 10–15 minutes.

Meanwhile prepare the glaze: Put the sugar and 100 ml (⅕ pt) of water in a pan. Bring to the boil and cook for a few minutes over a gentle heat. Remove from heat. Turn the kugelhopf on to a serving plate. Add the rum to the hot syrup and pour over the top and sides of the cake. Set the cake aside to get completely cold.

Note: This extremely delicious and light sweet can also be made with brandy, but in my view it is better with rum because of its rich aroma.

Croissants (Ragged rolls)

(makes about 20 croissants)

450 g	plain flour	1 lb
250–300 ml	milk	½ pt
150 g	butter	5 oz
50 g	castor sugar	2 oz
25 g	yeast	1 oz
	salt	

Cream the yeast with 3 tablespoons of lukewarm milk and 2 teaspoons of the sugar. Melt 30 g (1 oz) of the butter in a small pan. Sieve 400 g (1 lb) of the flour on to the work surface, add the remaining sugar, a pinch of salt, the yeast mixture, the melted butter and enough lukewarm milk to make a fairly stiff dough. Shape into a ball, place in a clean, floured bowl and make a cross in the dough with a knife (this speeds up the rising process). Cover with a clean kitchen cloth and leave in a warm place until it has doubled in size (2½–3 hours). Knock back on a floured surface and roll out until it is finger thickness. Place the remaining butter, softened and sliced approximately 3 mm (⅛ in) thick, in the middle of the dough. Fold over the ends of the dough to cover the butter. Fold over again, bang gently with the rolling pin, then roll out again and repeat the folding process. Put in a warm place for 25 minutes to rest. Roll out and fold a third time, then put aside to rest for another 15 minutes. Finally roll out the dough until it is approximately 5 mm (¼ in) thick. Cut into triangles with sides roughly 15 cm (6 in) long. Start at one side and roll up tightly to the opposite corner, then twist them round into a crescent shape. Arrange at some distance apart on a greased baking tray, cover with a kitchen cloth and leave in a warm place to rise for 1½–2 hours. Brush the tops with the remaining milk, warmed slightly. (They can also be sprinkled with a little sugar if you wish.) Bake in a preheated oven (200° C/400° F/Gas 6) for 10–15 minutes until golden brown. Leave to cool on the tray.

Variation: Before rolling up each croissant a little jam or thick vanilla cream can be spread on the dough.

Note: Rumour has it that this crescent-shaped roll, known all over the world by its French name "croissant" and accepted by all as French, is actually Hungarian in origin. Apparently in the Autumn of 1686 the soldiers, who had gathered together to recapture Buda which was in the hands of the Turks, were presented with crescent shaped rolls by the bakers of the town as sustenance and also to spur them on to a concerted effort in the ensuing battle. Even the most suspicious Turk would have failed to notice that the fires under the baker's ovens were bigger than usual. The crescent-shaped rolls mocked the Turkish emblem.

Chocolate soufflé

125 g	bitter plain chocolate	4½ oz
100 g	castor sugar	4 oz
45 g	butter or margarine	1½ oz
30 g	plain flour	1 oz
6	eggs	6
300 ml	milk	½ pt
2 pinches	bicarbonate of soda	2 pinches
	salt	

Melt the butter in a small pan, add the flour and make a light brown roux. Remove from heat and gradually add the warm milk, beating until smooth. Return to the heat and cook until it thickens stirring all the time, in much the same way as you make a Béchamel sauce. Put aside to cool slightly then beat in the egg yolks, one at a time, and a pinch of salt.

Melt the chocolate in a bowl over a pan of boiling water. Mix in the sugar and 1–2 tablespoons of water. When cool add to the egg mixture. Finally add the bicarbonate of soda and lightly fold in the stiffly beaten egg whites. Spoon the mixture into a greased fluted kugelhopf mould. Hit the bottom of the tin gently to remove any pockets of air. Bake in a preheated oven (180° C/350° F/Gas 4) for approximately 45 minutes. Test with a meat skewer.

Serve the soufflé immediately, otherwise it will collapse. Offer whipped cream.

Note: The soufflé is not as delicious if it is kept waiting so it should be prepared when the other courses can be timed exactly or when the guests are content to have a little rest between the main course and the sweet.

Chocolate cream

250 g	bitter chocolate	9 oz
8	egg whites	8
5	egg yolks	5
10 g	butter	2 tsp
4	sponge fingers	4
4 tbs	dark rum	4 tbs
100–200 ml	whipping cream	$^1/_5$–$^2/_5$ pt
1 tsp	vanilla sugar	1 tsp
	salt	

Melt the chocolate and butter in a bowl over a pan of boiling water. Remove from the heat and add the egg yolks one by one, beating vigorously. Put aside to cool. Meanwhile prepare 4 individual glass bowls. Break one sponge finger into each bowl and sprinkle with the rum. Whisk the egg whites until stiff and fold lightly into the cream. Spoon into the bowls. Cover and chill in the refrigerator for at least 3 hours, but not longer than 12.

Just before serving decorate with whipped cream flavoured with vanilla sugar and candied fruit, wafer biscuits or roasted nuts.

Note: This is well worth making for both children and adults. Everyone will love it. For children, just substitute 4 tbs fruit syrup for the rum.

Black doughnuts (Hungarian eclairs)

6 portions	cream puff mixture (see p. 61)	6 portions
500 ml	vanilla cream made with milk (see p. 62)	1 pt
150 g	plain chocolate glaze (see p. 62)	5 oz
200 ml	whipping cream	$^2/_5$ pt
10 g	vanilla sugar (see p. 60)	1 tsp

Grease a baking tray and dust with flour. Prepare the cream puff mixture following the recipe on page 61 then put aside to get quite cold. Put in a piping bag and pipe strips 10 cm (4 in) long on to the baking tray, some distance apart as they will

swell up during baking. Bake in a preheated oven (180° C/350° F/Gas 4) for 15–20 minutes until golden brown. Do not open the oven door for 15 minutes.

Leave to cool on the tray. Meanwhile prepare the vanilla cream and leave to cool. Spoon it into a piping bag and using the smallest nozzle fill the "slippers" with cream, by making a hole just big enough for the tip of the nozzle to fit in.

Arrange side-by-side on an oblong serving plate. Make the chocolate glaze and brush the top of each cake. Keep in the refrigerator until ready to use. Serve with whipped cream flavoured with the vanilla sugar.

Variation: Different flavoured cream can be used instead of vanilla (e. g. coffee or chocolate), in which case the cakes should be covered with a different glaze in a contrasting colour.

Profiteroles

6 portions	cream puff mixture (see p. 61)	6 portions
	for the cream	
150 g	icing sugar	5 oz
150 g	plain chocolate	5 oz
30 g	plain flour	1 oz
8	egg yolks	8
	a little butter	

Profiteroles

½	vanilla pod	½
500 ml	milk	1 pt
200–300 ml	whipping cream	⅖–½ pt

Make the cream puff mixture in the usual way then put aside to cool. Grease a baking tray and dust with flour. Spoon the mixture into a piping bag and using a plain nozzle pipe small balls about the size of a hazelnut on to the tray some distance apart. Bake in a preheated oven (180° C/350° F/Gas 4) for 15–20 minutes until golden brown. (Do not open the oven for 15 minutes.) Leave to cool on the tray. Put the milk into a pan, add the vanilla pod and bring to the boil. Cover with a lid to keep warm. Beat the egg yolks and sugar until thick and fluffy, then add flour and the milk a little at a time (remove the vanilla pod before adding the milk). Beat until smooth. Place over low heat or over a pan of boiling water and cook until it thickens stirring all the time. Remove from the heat. Add the melted chocolate and leave to cool. Whip the cream until thick, spoon into a piping bag and using the smallest nozzle make a tiny hole in each profiterole and fill with the cream. To serve carefully pile the profiteroles into a pyramid on a large serving dish (approximately 22–25 cm—8¾–9¾ in in diameter) and pour the chocolate cream in a thin stream over the top. Chill in the refrigerator for at least 1 hour to allow the cream to become firm. It is an impressive sight; ideal for really special occasions.

Rice soufflé with sultanas (Ricekoch)

(for 6–8 people)

750 ml	milk	1½ pts
100 g	butter or margarine	4 oz
150 g	castor sugar	5 oz
400 g	rice	1 lb
4	eggs, separated	4
100 g	sultanas	4 oz
	grated rind of 1 lemon, salt	
1 tbs	plain flour	1 tbs
	breadcrumbs	
	strongly flavoured jam	

Soak the sultanas in a small bowl with a little water. Put the milk, 250 ml (½ pt) water, the butter, sugar and a pinch of salt into a pan and bring to the boil. Add the washed rice and simmer until tender, stirring all the time (the rice should have absorbed all the liquid). Put aside to cool,

Layered roll pudding

then add the egg yolks, the sultanas—drained and dusted in flour, the grated lemon rind and lastly the stiffly beaten egg whites. Grease a round cake tin and dust with flour. Spoon in the mixture and bake in a preheated oven (180° C/350° F/Gas 4) for 40–45 minutes until golden brown. Serve warm or cold with the hot jam.
Note: This is very quick to prepare, inexpensive and very filling. It should follow a soup or a light main course. It is first and foremost a favourite among children.

Layered roll pudding

10	white rolls (preferably bridge roll shape)	10
1 litre	milk	2 pt
4	eggs	4
50 g	castor sugar	2 oz
¼	vanilla pod	¼
100 g	walnuts	4 oz
100 g	bottled sour cherries	4 oz
1 tbs	sour cherry jam	1 tbs
10 g	butter	2 tsp

Put the milk and vanilla pod into a pan and bring to the boil. Remove from the heat, cover with a lid and leave for 10 minutes before removing the pod.

Beat the egg yolks and sugar until thick and fluffy then gradually add the milk. Pour into a pan and simmer stirring all the time until it thickens. Do not bring to the boil.

Slice the rolls into rings of finger thickness. Pour over the hot milk and egg mixture and put aside until cool (the milk should be almost completely absorbed by the bread). Grease a deep, round fireproof dish and place a layer of "soaked" roll at the bottom, followed by a sprinkling of ground walnuts and a few stoned cherries. Continue the layers until all the ingredients are used up, finishing with a layer of sliced roll. Bake in a preheated oven (200–220° C/400–425° F/Gas 6–7) for approximately 35 minutes until the top is golden brown. Beat the egg whites with a pinch of salt until stiff, gently fold in the sour cherry jam and spread over the pudding. Return to the oven for a few minutes until the egg white is very pale brown. It is delicious served warm or cold.

Note: Ground poppyseeds can be used instead of walnuts. This is a highly recommended sweet after a light main course or a soup. It will be a great favourite with the children.

Hungarian pasta pudding

Hungarian pasta pudding

500 g	curd cheese	1¼ lb
300 g	plain flour	11 oz
200 g	icing sugar	7 oz
3	eggs	3
	salt, a little milk	
100 ml	soured cream	⅕ pt
50 g	sultanas	2 oz
50 g	blanched chopped almonds	2 oz
	grated rind of ½ lemon	
50 g	butter	2 oz
	breadcrumbs	

Soak the sultanas in warm milk, water or rum.

To prepare the pasta: Rub 150 g (5 oz) of the curd cheese through a hair sieve and mix with the flour. Add 1 egg, a pinch of salt and enough milk to make a fairly soft mixture. Shape into a ball, place on a well floured surface and roll out to a thickness of about 5 mm (¼ in). Cut into wide strips, then lay the strips one on top of the other, sprinkling a little flour in between each layer so that they do not stick. Then cut into thin strips approximately 1 cm (½ in) wide using a sharp knife. Cook in plenty of boiling water or milk for 5–7 minutes. Drain well and leave to cool.

When still slightly warm mix with the following *cream:* Cream the butter and icing sugar until light and fluffy. (The amount of sugar can be decreased according to taste.) Then beat in the 2 egg yolks, the soured cream, the almonds, grated lemon rind, drained sultanas, remaining curd cheese and lastly the stiffly beaten egg whites. Spoon over the pasta and mix lightly together. Grease a fireproof dish and sprinkle with breadcrumbs. Spoon in the pudding and bake in a preheated oven (180° C/350° F/Gas 4) for approximately 30 minutes. Serve immediately.

Hungarian sponge cake

(for 10–12 people)

3	sponge cakes, 1 plain, 1 walnut, and 1 chocolate	3

Hungarian sponge cake

	for the basic sauce	
200 g	castor sugar	7 oz
250 ml	water	½ pt
100 ml	dark rum	⅕ pt
¼	vanilla pod	¼
	grated rind of 1 lemon and 1 orange	
	for the vanilla cream	
500 ml	milk	1 pt
4	egg yolks	4
40 g	plain flour	1½ oz
15 g	gelatine	½ oz
	for the filling	
100 g	walnuts	4 oz
50 g	apricot jam	2 oz
1 tsp	cocoa	1 tsp
80 g	raisins or sultanas	3 oz
	for the chocolate sauce	
150 g	plain chocolate	5 oz
250 g	castor sugar	9 oz
150 ml	water	¼ pt
100 ml	dark rum	⅕ pt
400 ml	whipped cream	¾ pt

It is probably easier to buy ready made sponge cakes, but if you prefer to bake your own see page 61. You need 3 sponge cakes approximately 1 cm (½ in) thick. Mix all the ingredients for the *basic cream* together. Pour into a saucepan and cook over a low heat stirring constantly until it begins to thicken. Put aside to cool.

Make the vanilla cream in the usual way (see p. 62). Dissolve the gelatine in a little water and stir quickly into the hot cream. Put aside to cool, then keep refrigerated until ready to use.

For the chocolate sauce: Place the cubed chocolate, sugar, water and rum in a saucepan and heat over a low heat or a pan of boiling water until the chocolate has melted and the sauce is smooth. Put aside to cool. Soak the sultanas in a little water then drain well. Grind the walnuts.

Put the plain sponge cake on a deep serving plate. Sprinkle with some of the basic sauce. Spread half the vanilla cream on top, followed by half the walnuts and sultanas. Place the walnut sponge cake on top and repeat the procedure. Top with the chocolate cake and pour over the remaining basic sauce. Cover with apricot jam and then a little cocoa. Leave overnight in the refrigerator. When serving put several small spoonfuls of the pudding into individual glass or china bowls. Decorate with the whipped cream and pour the chocolate sauce over the top. It is now ready to eat.

Note: This sweet is known in Hungary as "Somlói galuska". It is not worthwhile making a smaller quantity, as it would not save you any time.

Salzburg pasta pudding

(for 6–8 people)

	for the pasta	
200 ml	milk	⅖ pt
100 g	butter	4 oz
200 g	plain flour	7 oz
4	egg yolks	4
	salt	
	for the filling	
150 ml	milk	¼ pt
½	vanilla pod	½
100 g	castor sugar	4 oz
3	eggs	3
60 g	plain flour	2 oz
50 g	blanched almonds	2 oz
50 g	sultanas	2 oz
10 g	butter	2 tsp
	vanilla sugar for dusting (see p. 60)	

Put the sultanas in a small bowl with a little warm milk or water and leave to soak. Make the pasta, following the recipe for cream puffs on page 61 and leave to cool. Put the milk, sugar and vanilla pod into a large pan and bring to the boil. Lower the heat, cut the pasta into small noodles and drop into the pan. Remove the noodles with a perforated spoon when they rise to the surface and drain in a colander. Strain the milk and remove the vanilla pod. Blend the egg yolks with the flour until smooth, then add the milk a little at a time. Place over a low heat or over a bowl of boiling water and stir constantly until it thickens. Remove from the heat and while still warm add the ground almonds, the drained sultanas, the noodles and finally the stiffly beaten egg whites. Spoon into a greased fireproof dish and bake in a preheated oven (180° C/350° F/Gas 4) for approximately 30 minutes until golden brown. Take care not to overcook the pudding, it should be soft and creamy inside. Dust with vanilla icing sugar and serve at once, otherwise it will collapse like a soufflé.

Slipped layered pancakes

	for the batter	
50 g	butter	2 oz
50 g	castor sugar	2 oz

50 g	plain flour	2 oz
5	eggs	5
300 ml	milk or single cream	½ pt
	grated rind of 1 orange and 1 lemon	
3 tbs	dark rum or orange liqueur	3 tbs
	salt	
	for the filling	
100 g	ground walnuts	4 oz
1 tsp	vanilla sugar (see p. 60)	1 tsp
150–200 g	apricot jam or marmalade	5–7 oz
	oil for frying	

Soften the butter, then add the 25 g (1 oz) of the sugar, and the egg yolks. Beat until thick and fluffy. Add the sifted flour then the milk or cream a little at a time, the grated lemon and orange rind, the salt and the rum or liqueur. Beat until smooth.

Whisk the egg whites and the rest of the sugar until stiff and fold into the batter.

Have a round fireproof dish ready to slip your pancakes into. Mix the vanilla icing sugar with the ground walnuts and place near the hob with the pot of marmalade or jam.

Pour a little oil into the pan and place over medium heat. Pour a spoonful of the batter into the pan, it should be approximately 1 cm (½ in) thick. Fry the bottom until it is golden brown, do not turn over, but with the help of a spatula or fish slice slip the pancake into the dish. Sprinkle the top with the ground walnut and sugar mixture and dot with a little jam or marmalade. Fry the next pancake and slip it on top of the first one then sprinkle again with the walnut and jam. Continue in the same way until you have used up all the batter (it should make 6–8 pancakes altogether. (Place the last pancake with the cooked side uppermost. Bake in a preheated oven (180° C/350° F/Gas 4) for 10–15 minutes. Make sure that you

Slipped layered pancakes

don't put it into a hotter oven otherwise it will spoil.

Dust the vanilla icing sugar before serving. Cut into wedges like a cake.

This is quite an undertaking but it is well worth the effort.

Fruit and cream pancakes

	for the batter	
250 g	plain flour	9 oz
3	eggs	3
500 ml	milk	1 pt
3 tbs	oil	3 tbs
	salt	
3 tbs	dark rum	3 tbs
	for the filling	
500 ml	milk for vanilla cream (see p. 62)	1 pt
300 g	bottled fruit	11 oz
	for the topping	
	icing sugar flavoured with cinnamon or cocoa	

Make pancakes following the recipe on page 61, but add the rum to the batter. Fry thin pancakes and keep warm.

Prepare the vanilla cream in the usual way. Stand in a pan of cold water to cool, stirring occasionally to stop a skin from forming on the top.

Drain the bottled or canned fruit (peaches, pineapple, pear, stoned cherries, mandarin oranges etc.), thoroughly, dice them and mix with the vanilla cream. Spread each pancake with cream, roll up and dust with the cinnamon or chocolate flavoured icing sugar. Serve immediately.

Note: These pancakes are ideal after a light main course or substantial soup. They are quite filling, so do not prepare more than 3 per person.

Gundel's pancakes

(for 6–8 people)

	for the batter	
250 g	plain flour	9 oz
3	eggs	3
500 ml	milk	1 pt
3 tbs	oil	3 tbs
	salt	
	for the filling	
200 g	ground walnuts	7 oz
200 g	icing sugar	7 oz
200 ml	single cream	²/₅ pt
	grated lemon rind	
50 g	sultanas	2 oz
	for the sauce	
100 g	plain chocolate	4 oz
3	egg yolks	3
approx. 250 ml	milk	½ pt
100 ml	whipping cream	⅕ pt
1 tsp	flour	1 tsp
¼	vanilla pod	¼
2–3 tbs	dark rum	2–3 tbs
	vanilla icing sugar for dusting (see p. 60)	

Put the sultanas into a small bowl with some water to soak. Before preparing the batter make the *sauce* in the following way: Put the milk, chocolate and vanilla pod into a pan and bring to the boil. Remove the vanilla. Beat the sugar, flour and egg yolks together until thick and fluffy then, stirring constantly, gradually add to the hot milk. Simmer or place over a pan of boiling water and cook until it is thick and creamy stirring all the time. Remove from the heat and add the rum and the whipped cream. Blend the sauce until smooth. Keep hot until ready to use.

Make the pancake batter in the usual way following the recipe on page 61. This quantity will make 12–15 pancakes. You should not allow more than 2 per person as they are very filling.

Mix the ground walnuts with the icing sugar, the lemon rind, the drained sultanas and cream. Fry the pancakes in the oil and spread each one with this mixture. Roll up or fold into four like a handkerchief. Pour a generous amount of sauce on top and dust with vanilla icing sugar.

Serve immediately. They are absolutely heavenly.

Note: When serving heat up a ladleful of rum, tilt the spoon so that the rum ignites, proceeding in the same way as you would if preparing a flambé dish. Pour the rum over the pancakes and serve.

Transylvanian curd cheese pancakes

	for the batter	
250 g	plain flour	9 oz
3	eggs	3
500 ml	milk	1 pt
3 tbs	oil	3 tbs
	salt	
	for the filling	
500 g	curd cheese	1¼ lb
2	eggs	2
100 g	vanilla icing sugar (see p. 60)	4 oz
	grated rind of 1 lemon	
50 g	sultanas	2 oz
	for the topping	
400 ml	soured cream	¾ pt
1	egg yolk	1
1 tsp	vanilla sugar (see p. 60)	1 tsp

Put the sultanas in a bowl with a little water and leave to soak. Prepare the batter in the usual way, following the recipe on page 61.

To make the filling: rub the curd cheese through a hair sieve and add the egg yolks, the sugar, lemon rind, the drained sultanas and lastly the stiffly beaten egg whites. Fry the pancakes in oil and spread each one with the filling. Roll up tightly and arrange in an oval fireproof dish in a row. Beat the soured cream with the egg yolk and vanilla sugar until frothy. Pour over the pancakes. Smooth the top and bake in a preheated oven (180° C/350° F/Gas 4) for approximately 20 minutes until the soured cream topping is golden brown.
Serve immediately.

Some useful tips

— Always *test cakes* and other baked goods by using meat skewers to see if they are cooked. To do this simply insert the skewer into the middle of the cake. If it comes out clean the cake is done. Temperatures in ovens do vary slightly, so you might find that your cake needs a little longer than I have suggested in the recipes. If the skewer does not come out absolutely clean, leave the cake for a further 5 minutes before testing it again. But be careful not to burn it.

— Nearly all *cakes* and *puddings* have to be baked in a preheated oven, so turn it on at least 10 minutes before you start baking.

— If the *oven* does not bake evenly it is advisable to line the cake tin with greaseproof paper and to grease the paper. If the top of the cake or pudding is getting brown before it has cooked right through, cover it loosely with kitchen foil.

— It is a good idea to keep a *wooden spoon* which is used only for the preparation of sweet cakes and puddings. Unless otherwise stated, always allow cakes to cool on wire racks to prevent the bottom from getting soggy. Allow cakes to get absolutely cold before filling them with cream, unless otherwise stated.

— Stir *cooked creams* frequently while they are cooling, to prevent a skin from forming on the top.

— Always sieve *flour* and *icing sugar*.

— Break *eggs* separately into a small cup before adding to the mixture. Beat them into the mixture one at a time.

— A pinch of *salt* improves the flavour of cakes and puddings.

— Always cream fresh *yeast* with a little lukewarm milk or water and leave to ferment before adding to the other ingredients. A little sugar may be added to the liquid when dried yeast is used.

— Add *baking powder* to the flour or dissolve in a little liquid to enable it to become evenly distributed.

— Wash and dry *oranges and lemons* thoroughly before grating the rind.

— *Lemons* and *oranges* will be juicier if you put them in warm water for a few minutes before slicing.

— Soak *sultanas* for 1–2 hours in warm water, milk or alcohol. Then drain well and dust with flour. Shake off any excess flour using a perforated spoon or a sieve. This will stop the sultanas from sinking to the bottom.

— This process is also recommended for *candied fruit*.

— Always peel *almonds* and *hazelnuts* before adding to a sweet. Blanch almonds in boiling water. Drain them then peel. You will find that the skin will come off with the greatest of ease. Place the almonds on a clean cloth to dry or put in a cool oven for a few minutes.

— Roast *hazelnuts* in a frying pan until golden brown. Leave to cool then rub off the skin between the palms of the hands.

— Add a pinch of salt to *egg whites* to make them really stiff when beaten.

— To obtain *stiffly whipped cream* always use very fresh cream and chill it thoroughly before whipping.

— Only add *gelatine* to creams of various kinds when it has completely dissolved. This process can be speeded up if the gelatine and water is brought slowly to the boil over a low heat, but allow it to cool slightly before beating into the cream.

— Brush the edges of *cream-filled puff pastry* slices with water and press them gently together otherwise the cream will come out during baking. Better still rub an ice cube along the edges.

— To ensure that you get *evenly sliced cakes* for sandwiching together, place a piece of thin white sewing cotton round the cake at the desired place, tie knots at each end and then gently pull the cotton until the cake is cut.

— To make sure that *layered cakes*, especially fluted ones, can be put back in their original position, push a tooth-pick into the side of each layer in a vertical line before you lift off the layers.

— The *appearance* of a cake is very important, so take care when slicing them and arranging them on a serving plate. Do not cover the golden brown sides of the cake with *icing sugar* unless stated otherwise.

— When *storing* a cake or pudding in the refrigerator be sure to wrap it carefully in kitchen foil or cling film or cover it with a bowl to prevent it from being tainted by other food odours.

— Success depends on your keeping strictly to the given quantities and following the instructions carefully.

Before you begin make sure that you have everything prepared in advance—the ingredients, equipment, cake tin etc. This will speed up your work and help keep the kitchen tidy.

— Take the *butter* or *margarine* out of the refrigerator well in advance to enable it to soften and thereby become easier to work with.

— *To make vanilla sugar:* Put 1 or 2 vanilla pods into a screw top jar or tin. Fill the jar with icing sugar, to cover the pods. As you use the sugar, replenish the jar. Vanilla-flavoured castor sugar can be made in the same way.

— *Store spices* like cinnamon, cloves, aniseed etc.

in dark screw top jars, otherwise they will lose their aroma and colour.

— Add a little castor sugar when roughly *chopping almonds* or *hazelnuts*. This will stop the pieces from "flying" off the table. (Remember to use that much less in the recipe.)

— *Walnuts, almonds* and *hazelnuts* will not go rancid if kept in their shells until you need them. Be careful when buying shelled nuts, particularly towards the end of spring and early summer. Make sure that they have a fresh smell, otherwise your cakes will be ruined.

— Carefully pick out any bits of shell before chopping or grinding nuts. If you fail to do this you might end up with a broken grinder, a broken knife or even worse—a broken tooth!

— If *old honey* or *jam crystallizes* boil up with a little water and they will be as good as new. The jam, however, must be kept in the refrigerator or it might go mouldy. I am afraid the only thing to do if a pot of jam does go mouldy is simply to throw it away. The rest of the jam will be infected, even if the mould is only visible on the top.

Plain sandwich cake and variations

6	eggs	6
175 g	castor sugar	6 oz
175 g	plain flour	6 oz
	grated rind of ½ lemon	
	salt	

Beat the egg yolks and sugar until thick and fluffy. Mix the lemon rind with the flour then fold into the egg yolk mixture alternating with the stiffly beaten egg whites, to which a pinch of salt has been added. When blending in the egg whites and flour use a perforated wooden spoon or a hand whisk. Grease the bottom of a round sandwich tin and dust with flour. (Do not grease the sides otherwise the cake will rise in the middle and not have a nice flat top.) Pour in the cake mixture and bake in a preheated oven (180° C/350° F/Gas 4) for 40 minutes. Do not open the oven door for the first 30 minutes as the cake will flop. When cooked leave in the oven for 5–8 minutes with the door ajar. (The great difference in temperature can also cause the cake to collapse.)

Leave to cool in the tin for a few minutes, then turn out on to a wire rack. Leave to get absolutely cold before filling.

Swiss roll is made following the same recipe, except that a rectangular sandwich tin is used instead. The baking time is much shorter for Swiss rolls—15–20 minutes altogether. When cooked turn out straight away on to a clean kitchen cloth. Spread with cream and roll up tightly while still hot.

Walnut or chocolate sandwich cake

Follow the recipe for plain sandwich cake but add ground walnuts or cocoa. Decrease the amount of flour by the amount of ground walnuts or cocoa used.

Economical sponge cake

This is a much lighter cake which uses few eggs.

4	eggs	4
250 g	icing sugar	9 oz
9 tbs	water	9 tbs
150 g	plain flour	5 oz
2 heaped tsp	baking powder	2 heaped tsp

Beat the egg yolks with the icing sugar until thick and fluffy.
Add the water a spoonful at a time, then the sieved flour and baking powder. Finally fold in the stiffly beaten egg whites.

Basic cream puff recipe (Hungarian choux pastry)

80 g	butter or margarine	3 oz
110 g	plain flour	4 oz
5	eggs	5
	salt	

Put the butter, a pinch of salt and 100 ml (4 fl oz) water in a pan and bring to the boil. Add all the flour, beating vigorously then continue cooking over a low heat, stirring all the time until the mixture comes away from the sides of the pan. Remove from the heat and when cool beat in 4 of the eggs one at a time. It is very important to beat the mixture thoroughly as this will make the cream puffs light and aerated.

Grease a baking tray and then follow the recipe you have chosen (making big or small mounds or strips.) Leave to rest for 30 minutes then brush with the remaining beaten egg. Make sure that none of the egg drips down the sides on to the tray; as it will prevent the cakes from rising. Bake in a preheated oven (200–220° C/400–425° F/Gas 6–7) for 20–25 minutes until golden brown. Do not open the oven door for the first 20 minutes otherwise the cakes will flop. Leave to cool before filling according to the recipe.
Note: This quantity makes 4 portions. If you want to prepare more, increase the ingredients proportionately.

Pancakes (basic recipe)

250 g	plain flour	9 oz
3	eggs	3
500 ml	milk	1 pt
3 tbs	oil	3 tbs
	salt	

Sieve the flour into a large bowl. Make a well in the middle and add the eggs, oil and a pinch of salt. Beat until smooth then gradually add the milk. It is important to leave the batter to rest for at least an hour. Brush a large frying pan (with a diameter of roughly 20 cm–8 in) with a little oil. If you are using a non-stick pan it is unnecessary to use any oil as there is oil in the batter. Tip the pan so that the batter covers the bottom evenly. Fry over a high heat for a few seconds. Shake the pan and turn the pancake over with a palette knife or by tossing it in the air. Fry the other side then slip the pancake on to a plate and keep hot over a pan of boiling water.
Note: Pancake batter can be made with half milk and half soda or mineral water. The thinner you make the batter, the thinner the pancakes will be. It is advisable to learn how to turn pancakes over by tossing them in the air, particularly if you are using a non-stick pan as the surface might get damaged. Teflon-coated spatulas are obtainable and are recommended for use with non-stick frying pans. A non-stick pan is preferable to an ordinary one, because no oil is required and cooking fumes are therefore reduced.
Pancakes are even more delicious if a tablespoon of rum is added to the batter just before frying.

COOKED CREAMS

Vanilla cream (basic recipe)

4	egg yolks	4
75 g	plain flour	3 oz
150 g	castor sugar	5 oz
500 ml	milk	1 pt
½	vanilla pod or	½
1 tsp	vanilla sugar (see p. 60) lemon rind	1 tsp

Bring the milk to the boil with the vanilla and 1–2 pieces of lemon rind. Then put aside to cool. Meanwhile beat the egg yolks, sugar and flour until thick and frothy. Add the strained milk, then pour into a clean saucepan and cook over a low heat or over a pan of boiling water until it thickens, stirring all the time. Put aside to cool, stirring occasionally to prevent a skin from forming on the top.

Chocolate, coffee or caramel cream

Follow the recipe for vanilla cream, but for the chocolate cream add 80–100 g (3–4 oz) of crumbled *plain chocolate* to the boiling milk and stir until melted;
— add 30 g (1 oz) *cocoa* to the egg yolks.
For the coffee cream add 100 ml (⅕ pt) of very strong espresso *coffee* or 2 heaped tablespoons of instant coffee to the boiling milk.
For the *caramel* cream caramelize 50 g (2 oz) castor sugar in a pan then add the milk and bring to the boil. Use only 100 g (4 oz) of sugar with the egg yolks.
Note: The amount of sugar can be decreased according to taste.

Hot chocolate sauce

(for pancakes, soufflés and plain cakes)

100 g	plain chocolate	4 oz
100 g	icing sugar	4 oz
3	egg yolks	3
approx. 250 ml	milk	½ pt

100 ml	whipping cream	⅕ pt
1 tsp	plain flour	1 tsp
½	vanilla pod	½
2–3 tbs	dark rum	2–3 tbs

Pour the milk into a pan. Add the broken chocolate and vanilla pod, and bring to the boil. Remove the vanilla pod. Beat the sugar, flour and egg yolks until thick and frothy then gradually add the hot milk stirring all the time. Pour into a pan and simmer over a low heat or over boiling water until thick and creamy stirring constantly. Remove from heat and pour in the rum. Carefully add the whipped cream and stir until smooth.
Keep warm until ready to serve by standing it in a bowl of hot water.

Sugar glaze (simple, basic recipe)

250 g	icing sugar	9 oz
1–2 tbs	water	1–2 tbs

Put the sugar into a small pan and add 1–2 tablespoons of water. Simmer, stirring constantly, for a few minutes until the sugar has completely dissolved. Do not bring to the boil. Spread the syrup over the cake while it is still hot. The top and sides of the cake should be evenly covered.
Sugar glaze in its basic form is rarely used but the following ingredients can be added to make it more interesting:
— vanilla sugar;
— part water and part liqueur, orange juice or strong black coffee.
— Food colouring can be added, but only a few drops, as glazes with a strong colour do not look attractive.
Note: In order to make the glaze smooth and shining, pop the glazed cake into a cool, turned-off oven for a few minutes.

Royal glaze

250 g	icing sugar	9 oz
1	egg white	1
	a few drops lemon juice	

Sieve the icing sugar into a bowl and gradually add the stiffly beaten egg white. Beat thoroughly then add the lemon juice. It is unnecessary to cook this glaze, and it can be used in the same way as the others.

Chocolate glaze made with plain chocolate

150 g	plain chocolate	5 oz
70 g	icing sugar	3 oz
2	egg whites	2

Melt the chocolate in a bowl over boiling water, then beat in the icing sugar. Remove from the heat and beat with the egg whites until thick and creamy. Spread over the cake immediately and place in a cool, turned-off oven for a few minutes.

Wine sauce

(for 6–8 people)

300 ml	sweet white wine	½ pt
100 g	castor sugar	4 oz
4	eggs	4
1 tsp	vanilla sugar (see p. 60)	1 tsp
1–2	small pieces lemon rind	1–2
1 level tbs	plain flour	1 level tbs
	salt	

Beat the egg yolks with the flour, vanilla sugar and half the castor sugar until thick and frothy. Gradually pour in the wine, add the lemon and heat over a pan of boiling water. Stir constantly until it thickens. Do not bring to the boil, because the egg will curdle. Remove from the heat and carefully fold in the stiffly beaten egg whites to which a pinch of salt has been added. Remove the lemon rind and serve hot or slightly warm.

Cooking over steam

It is very important with many cooked creams to thicken them over a pan of boiling water and not over direct heat. The ideal thing for this operation is a double saucepan (double boiler) or two pans, one smaller than the other so that the small pan can be placed inside the bigger one. Add enough water to reach halfway up the larger pan. Bring the water to the boil and then keep it at boiling point over a low heat.
Stir constantly when thickening creams. This does take a little time, but it is unavoidable as the cream will be ruined if it gets too hot.

Some advice on the preparation of soufflés

The soufflé mixture can be prepared in advance, except for the addition of the stiffly beaten egg whites which must be folded in at the last minute when the oven has reached the right temperature and the soufflé dish is ready.
Increase the temperature of the oven slightly just after the soufflé has been put in.
Do not open the oven door for the first 20 minutes. After removing from the oven, prick the soufflé in 2 or 3 places to allow the steam to escape and to prevent the soufflé from flopping.
There are 2 ways of turning out a soufflé:
1. wait for a few minutes for the soufflé to shrink slightly, or
2. plunge the dish into warm water for a second or two, taking care not to drip water on the soufflé. I think the latter is the quicker way of doing it. Soufflés should be served immediately.

How can one tell if an egg is fresh or not?

It is essential to use really fresh eggs for cakes and puddings. One way of finding out if they are fresh is to pour 450 ml (¾ pt) of water into a large glass bowl and dissolve 60 g (2½ oz) of salt in it. Place an egg in a spoon and lower it into the bowl.
If it is fresh it will stay on the bottom in a horizontal position.
If it is two weeks old or older, it will rise to the surface.
If it is about 10 days old, it will float about midway. For making cakes use only really fresh eggs, otherwise they will fail.
The not-so-fresh eggs are still very good for savoury egg dishes.